SWEET

Suffolk Voices from the Past

Sydney Higgins

Alldrama
through Create Space

Sydney Higgins

'In those days, we used to eat all kinds of things – sweet sorrel. They did grow wild in the hedgerows. We used to eat the leaves of those.'

David Peachey

SWEET SORREL:
SUFFOLK VOICES FROM THE PAST

Create Space, 7290 Investment Drive, North Charleston, 29418, U.S.A.

Copyright © 2014 Sydney Higgins

All rights reserved.
No part of this publication may be reproduced, stored in a retrieval system or transmitted, in any form or by any means, electronic, mechanical, photocopying, recording or otherwise, without the prior permission of the author.

Library of Congress Control Number: 2013915490
ISBN-13: 9781491226728
ISBN-10: 1491226722

In Memoriam

Arthur Boast, Charlie Fisk, Cooker Carver, David Peachey, 'Granny Mill' Ashwell, Hector Moore, Jack Steele, Kate Middleditch, Ivy Burrell, Ruby Peachey & Russell Podd.

Author's Note

Although the rural Suffolk dialect is rapidly disappearing, all the people who speak in these pages used it. To make their words easier to read, they have not been written phonetically. For example, *I'll* has been retained but was pronounced *oi'll*. Most words ending with *-ing* (such as *working*) normally appear in the text as *workin'* but were pronounced *worken*.

Apart from these modifications, I have made no changes nor added anything to the words used by the people who spoke to me so many years ago. What remains is what they said. When they speak, it is their voice you can hear – not mine.

Sydney Higgins

CONTENTS

Preface	vii
The Blacksmith	9
Farm Labourers	29
The Servants	47
Suffolk Farmhouse Recipes	63
Poverty & the Poacher	75
Village Pubs	99
The Thatcher	121
Postscript	133
About the Author	141

Linocuts: Liz Cope pp. i, vi, 27, 62, 109, 116, 131

Cover Design: John Grain

Photographs: Sydney Higgins pp. viii, 9, 10, 14, 15, 19, 20, 23, 25, 44, 47, 98, 107, 115, 119, 120, 121, 122, 123, 124, 125, 126, 127, 128, 132, 133, 134, 139.

All other illustrations are in the public domain in those countries with a copyright term of life of the author plus 100 years or less.

Preface

For over twenty years, my wife and I, with our three sons, were fortunate enough to live in several Suffolk villages – Marlesford, Worlingworth, Bedfield, Debenham and Framlingham. At the time, we were among the small minority that had not been born and grown up in the area.

At first, I found the strong local dialect of the old men almost impossible to understand but, in time, I was able to talk to them and, more importantly, listen to what they had to say – their fascinating stories and accounts of their lives and experiences.

During that period, I was spending much of my time writing biographies and books for children. Whenever I could, I escaped to one or other of the many local pubs to enjoy the company of the cloth-capped farmhands as they told their tales, danced and sang.

One day, I was told that one of the old regulars had unexpectedly died. I was sad and, when I went to his funeral, I realised that his memories of the previous eighty years, his knowledge of apparently hundreds of songs and the story of his life had died with him. It was then I decided that I should start recording and transcribing the memories of some of the fascinating men and women I knew in rural Suffolk. This I did occasionally between 1976 and 1980. It was not then my intention that I should use the recordings to write a book. Other people, including most notably George Ewart Evans and Ronald Blythe, had already done that.

Time passed. Years later but over twenty-five years ago, my wife and I moved to Italy and brought with us most - although by no means all - of our possessions. A few months ago, the wife of my deceased literary agent, Andrew Best, visited us and asked what had happened to the recordings I had made. I did a search through some of the still unpacked boxes stored at the back of the garage. Much to my surprise and delight, I found the compact cassettes I'd used to make the recordings. To my dismay, all the tapes had withered and were unusable. Fortunately, the typed transcripts had survived - although some parts had been nibbled away by a hungry mouse.

As I read through the pages, I became aware that, although all the speakers had died years ago, their voices from the past, their songs and their recipes had survived and were demanding to be heard. *Sweet Sorrel* records what they had to say.

The Blacksmith

Hector Moore - born 1923

In most rural communities, the blacksmith was traditionally held in awe by almost all the other villagers who relied upon his skills not only to shoe horses but also to make and repair most of their agricultural machinery.

Usually the craft and its mysteries were passed from one generation to another in the same family. It is then not surprising that these masters of fire and iron were usually both physically strong and extremely independent. Indeed, many country people considered they had magical powers – a belief that the blacksmiths did little to discourage. Indeed, the livery of the Worshipful Company of Farriers includes three horseshoes pointing downwards. For others, this is a symbol of ill fortune.

Today, wrought iron, the metal most used by the old blacksmiths, is no longer produced commercially. Materials that are lighter and stronger have replaced it. For centuries, there was a blacksmith in almost every village. Now few are left and the traditional and important role played by the blacksmith in rural communities has all but disappeared.

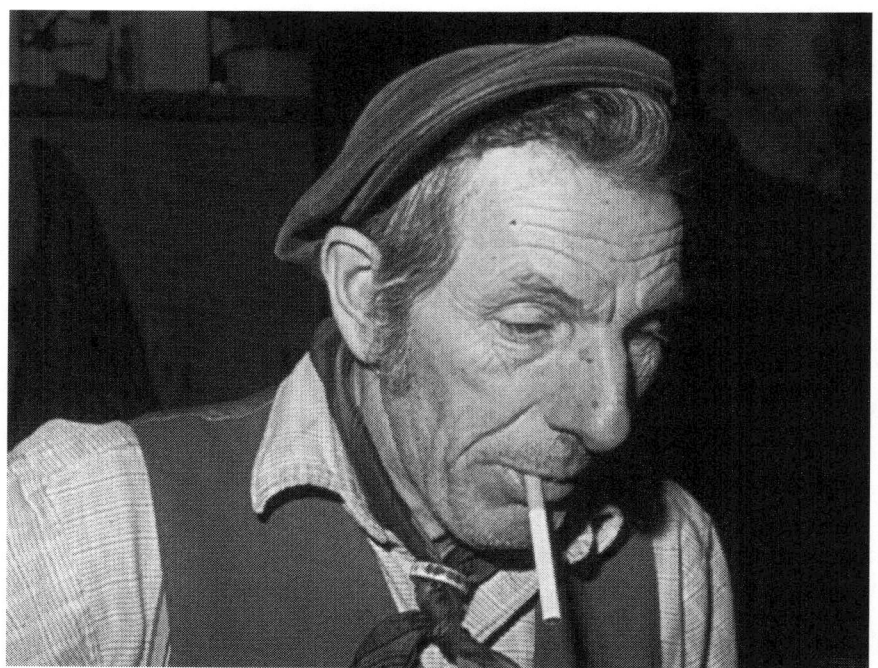

In 1980, when I interviewed Hector Moore he was the most famous blacksmith in the area. For over forty years, he had worked at his forge in Brandeston. Imbued with great dignity, pride and an immense love of his craft, he was truly 'one of Nature's gentlemen'. One sharp winter's evening, I visited him in his cottage next to the forge where he spoke about his life and work.

To me, school meant nothin'. I didn't want to know nothin' about school. The sooner I got out of school the better. I'd set my heart on what I wanted to do and I knew where I wanted to start and I knew where I wanted to finish in life. The only way you can achieve that is by educating yourself and not let other people educate you. You don't want to know what happened in 1066 to shoe horses, do you? But you want to know what happen inside the horse's head and nobody can teach you that at school. I can't hardly read nor write and don't want. But so long as you know how to make a living, that's the main thing, i'n't it?

So when did you decide that you wanted to be a blacksmith?

Before ever I left school. But I should have liked to have been a vet – that's what I should have liked to have been. But there was no grants, no subsidies, no university grants, was there? And no money! I mean if you had a bit of bread and butter, you had bread and butter. You never had bread, butter and jam. If you had bread and jam, you left the butter out. So there was no chance of ever being a vet then. There wa'n't the money to do it with. So that's why I'm so interested in horses in connection with my job. I'm as interested with the top half as I am with the bottom.

Mind you, all the farriers (that's a blacksmith who only shoes horses) were much more like vets. All the old farriers' books deal with horse diseases – there's very little about shoeing horses.

Then I suppose some men specialised in curing horses while others spent their time more in shoeing them. And I can remember when there was men about who were called horse-doctors. They were men which hadn't passed the veterinary certificate. I can remember one up unto, I suppose, the late forties. They were all known as horse-doctors. They did it full time and they did all the care of the horses. Then they got the same as we are. We aren't allowed to practice without a license. You aren't allowed to shoe a horse if you haven't got a license. Same as vets, you see.

But you did come from a family of blacksmiths, didn't you?

Yes, it's been in the family, we know from the records, back to 1760 on these premises. So there is, I suppose, a certain amount of it in the blood – if that can happen. I don't know whether it can, I'm sure. So I suppose I had a bit of a start. And yet why should that be me and not me other three brothers? So whether that's got any bearing on it, I wouldn't know.

So how old were you when you left school?

Fourteen. And I came straight here – started on the 2nd August 1937.

And presumably you had an apprenticeship?

Well I had rather an unfortunate beginning, because I started an apprenticeship with Charlie Bedfield, which worked with me grandparents, and he was retiring age in 1941. That was during the war and that left me here alone. So I hadn't finished me apprenticeship and what I didn't know then I had to find out for meself, because no-one'd tell you anything. All these things were closely guarded. So I didn't actually finish my apprenticeship. So I had a bit of a rough start and I managed this shop for me grandparent, or really for my grandmother – she was th'only one alive then – from '41 till she died in '47. So I managed it for six years and then it was left to me.

So how did you set about acquiring the information you needed?

I had to find things out by being like the three monkeys – eyes and ears open and mouth shut. Now if you could git tuppence to git into t' pub and git the half pint of beer and if you'd got another tuppence to buy a half-pint for somebody else – an old horseman – and sit right quiet, well that's where you used to git your knowledge from. And I spent a lot of time in the pub. And people used to say, 'Look, the silly fool!' But they didn't know what I was doing. I didn't go in a pub to drink beer. I went in t' educate meself, which was a rare lot pleasanter than sitting in the school. Ah, yes!

Mind, when I first started, I got 2/6p a week and me father said, 'We can't afford to keep you on that sort of money.' So I also used to look after a hundred and sixty pigs at the farm just down the road in the morning before I started here at six. I used to do a day's work – that was from six to six – and I used to look after 'em pigs ag'in when I went on the way home. And I got a penny a pig a week. And all the water was carried out of the pond with a pail. There wa'n't no such things as pumps. And I got a penny a pig a week for that – when I was fourteen.

But that work wa'n't unusual. The normal working week was fifty-six hours and, for that, a qualified tradesman was gitting twenty-eight shillings. That was sixpence an hour. And they say today things are dear. I mean that's a lot of nonsense. When we's talking about them time, Players cigarettes were sixpence for ten and eleven pence ha'p'ny for twenty and a man had got to work an hour to buy ten Players. Now how many Players can he buy today for an hour's wages? He can buy eighty, can't he?

Sam Friend, a wonderful old horseman at Cretingham, he told me th'old suit he wore – with horseshoe buttons and rows and rows of stitched – that cost him ten weeks' wages. Now you can git a funny suit today for ten weeks' wages, can't you? There's no comparison at all. And people say things are dear. They aren't dear! The only reason they seem dear is because we all got our priorities wrong, ain't we? I mean, if we could go back and live today exactly as I was living when I started work, we should be a millionaire!

But how then, when you worked such long hours, did you find the time to go into the pub to get the information you wanted?

Well you made the time. The young uns today can't work. They don't know the first thing about work. I mean, when you used to go home, yer hands was raw with blisters from the hot iron, 'cause that was all done with a sledge-hammer, beatin' it out. Old horseshoes, you used to weld one and a half together to make one new one. Material was dear then and labour was nothin', was it? I mean you never threw nothin' away. Old cart tyres you'd split 'em in half and make a pair of shoes. You never wasted a thing.

But there were people around – the gentry – who did have plenty. How did you feel about them?

You were brought up to respect them, weren't you? They were employing half the people in the village, weren't they? They were giving them bread and butter. They were the people that were finding the work. Mind, the majority of farmers were as poor as the men that worked for 'em. But you could always tell a good farmer, because his horses always looked well. 'Cause he knew that they was his livelihood. They always said, 'If poverty got into the stable, it got indoors.' And that was right. If you see a pair of horses that were all bone, they hadn't got a lot on the table indoors. No!

So how have things changed during your long career as a blacksmith?

Ninety per cent of the horses what are bred today, if they were put into work, they'd be dead within six months. They're bred wrong. They're bred too fine. They're too delicate. They've got to be wrapped in cotton wool. Half of them are like two nine-inch boards clapped together, aren't they? These horses here today, they can't work. They don't know what work is.

The horses years ago had to go out into the field at seven o'clock in the morning and they used to go what they called 'a journey' and they used to stop there till half past three. They never stopped for lunch and then they'd come back into the stable. The horse was always fed, watered and made comfortable and then, after, the man went home for his dinner. He didn't go home before all of that was finished. He'd go home probably at four, have his dinner and come back to make the horses comfortable for the night. And that was his day's work. Them horses, they never had a drop to drink from seven in the morning till they got home at night. Nor didn't the man. Pouring with rain, dusn't go home 'cos he'd get the sack. No, it was a hard life. But everybody was happy.

So which do you prefer – now or the way things were?

Oh, the way things were! I can prove that. When I started here all the accounts went out yearly, once a year at Christmas. And sometimes they went 'account rendered', which meant it was two years past. But the bank balance was always in the black, because you couldn't borrow money. Now, you send yer bills out every month but you've got to borrow money to bloody live. There must be something wrong! Certainly it was better before. Everybody today think the world owe them a living. I say we owe the world one, don't we? We want to be thankful to be here.

That wouldn't worry me a tinker's damn if I never set foot no more on that road out there. Everything I want I've got. I've got a job I like. My work is my hobby and I enjoy every minute of it. I've got a roof over the top - however humble. We've got a few cobwebs which I enjoy seeing. We've got a mess and a muddle. But I'm content – happy. What more do you want? I've got good health. I've got forty-three years at work and never a day in bed. I've only ever had but one week's holiday and that bloody near killed me! My philosophy of life is do six days a week and please yerself on the seventh. If everybody done that, this'd be a rare bit better place to live in.

This is an area still full of real old characters - many of them old horsemen. I know you've got fascinating tales about them. Can you please tell me some?

Well, there was Old Jack Capon. He worked a farm along the road here. He'd got an old Suffolk horse there that was a bit of a lad. He was a little bit spiteful at times and he wasn't against giving you one!

I was shoeing him one morning and the postman had left his bike outside the shop door and 'ad gone up the meadow. Well, I was shoeing this old horse. Well, he fly at me and I hit him a-top the tail with a hammer. I never said nothin'. Jack was leaning up against the wall, holding a rope, sucking an old clay pipe. When I hit this horse that frightened it and it jumped right out of the shop. That hit the bike. Over it went. That horse hopped on that three times. That frightened it again and it jumped back into the shop.

Jack still stood there sucking his pipe – never moved! He say, 'Blast, boy! He's some fit, isn't he?'

That's all he said. We got on with the job. The postman had to carry the bike home. He couldn't do a thing about it. It was Post Office property and he shouldn't have left it there!

* * *

Old John Fairweather at harvest time had got a pair of horses in the waggon, loaded with corn. He worked for an old man with a stiff leg. He was going through the gateway with this load of corn and the waggon slipped into the ditch. The whole lot went – the horses and waggon – right into the ditch.

His governor come stomping across the meadow.

Old John, he stood there and said, 'You want to look out, master! We're goin' to have a bloody mess here in a minute!'

*   *   *

Horses get a complaint we call laminitis - that's foot trouble through over-feeding of rich oats. Now poor Metty Rose was a thatcher and he never was too good on his feet – lot of ladder work, you see.

When he thatched this house here, he used to have his dinner in the shop with us. He always had an old two-pound sugar bag full of Quaker Oats and half a pound of farm butter – that was his dinner. He'd have a spoonful of oats and then a bit of butter. That went on several days.

Then, one day, I see he hadn't got it. So I said, 'You've changed your diet, Metty!'

He say, 'Yes. I gone on to these 'ere Weetabix. Used to have Quaker Oats but they didn't suit me old feet!'

You see, knowing about horses, he thought that eating too many oats were bad for his feet!

*   *   *

There was an old man lived in Kettleborough in the little old cottage beside the road and he always used to sit with the door on the jar with a stick propped behind it to keep it half open.

One day, this old roadster shot his head round the door and say, 'What's the time, mate?'

Old Minns struck him on the skull with the stick and he says, 'It's now struck one!'

The roadster shook his head and says, 'It's a bloody good job I didn't ask an hour ago!'

* * *

One evening, Jack Cooper's governor told him to put four horses in the waggon the next morning and then go to the miller's and get a load of corn. Of course, he meant that the horses should be harnessed to pull the waggon.

Old Jack thought he'd have a skit with the governor. So he drew the waggon up beside the muck-hill and led the four horses on top the muckle. Then, from there, he led two of them so they were standing on top the waggon and the other two were still stood on top the muckle.

He went and knocked the governor up. It was about five in the mornin'. 'Can't get all them horses in the waggon, master,' he says.

'What!' the governor said. 'Call yerself a bloody horseman! Can't put four horses in a waggon!'

Course, the old man come stumpin' out and there stood these horse – two atop the waggon and two on the muckle.

Jack said, 'Are you going to put the other two in?'

Course, he did all that just to prove what a good horseman he was, 'cos you've got to be a bloody good horseman to get two horses to stand in a waggon!

Well that brings us nicely to horses and the important question of how you manage to control them so successfully. What is the secret?

We were always taught that there's no such thing as a bad horse or a bad child. Thar's bad horsemen and bad parents. You see, a horse is never born. He's always made. When he's born, he's an animal. He's always made and he turn out what you make him. And if you've got a bad horseman, he'll have a bad horse.

To master these horses, you've got to try and think the same as they do. You've got to get inside them. You've got to be there the whole time. If you could see a horse twenty-five hours a day and eight days a week and fifty-three weeks a year, that's a tremendous help! The longer you can be with the animal, certainly the better results you get. These old horsemen used to sit up all night with them if they got a bad one. But when you're shoeing the horse, you only see him six hours a year. So you've got to do it by not being with them all the time.

But I'm positive you can think a horse into doing anything. If you get a bad horse – and I've proved it in my case by shoeing them, not working 'em or anything – you can keep him in your mind the whole time and be with him if he's ten mile away. There's no need to be near him. I'm positive that it works. If I know a bad horse is coming, I start thinking about him and try to get inside him before ever he get here. If I've got a bad horse, I'd rather be with that alone. I don't want anybody with it. I need to be with it on me own.

It's the same with shoeing a horse. If I'm shoeing it, there can be a lot of people standin' and look at me and I don't say a word to them. I must be inside that horse the whole time. I don't think there's many people can do it but, once you have won a horse's confidence, you're there. You're in control.

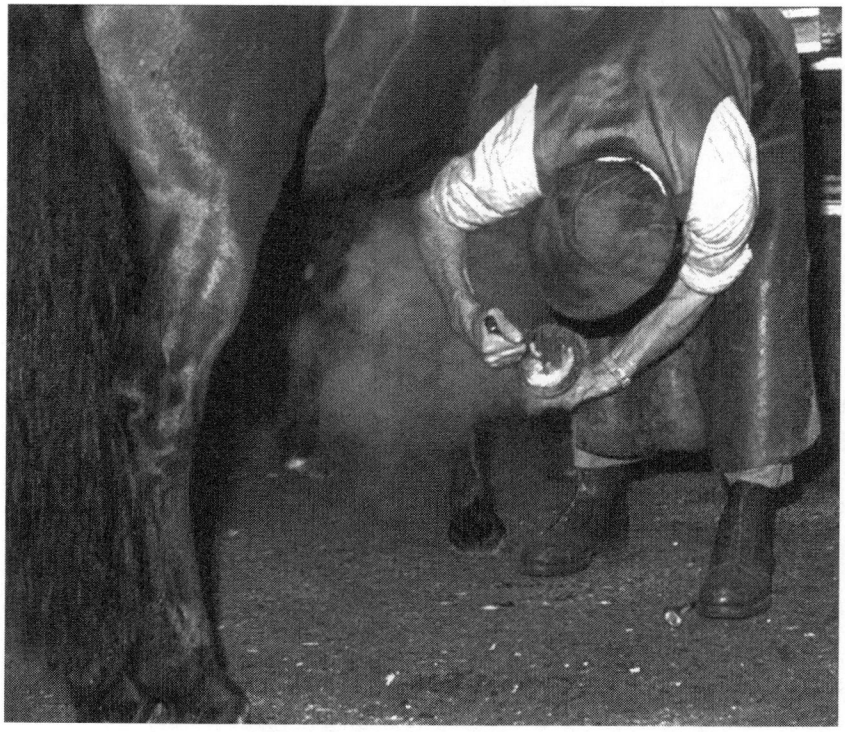

I have been told that blacksmiths had a special bone of a toad or frog that was thought to have an almost magical power over horses. Could you tell me something about it?

Well that's a thing you don't go into too deeply because that probably involves witchcraft. I've got one which I never show anybody and I never talk about it. That is a thing which is used but, if you're not careful with 'em, they can be a bit troublesome.

There's a bit of a ritual to get this bone. There's one or two different ways of doing it. The most popular is you get the frog and you stick it on a blackthorn bush alive and leave it there till it dies. Then you have to wait until there's a full moon and then you take off the whole skeleton and you put it in a running stream. And there's one bone which will go up-stream. It may seem impossible to believe but it's true.

But that is one of those things that people don't like talking about and a lot of the old horsemen would never let their wives know they'd got one in case there was any misfortune in the household that would be blamed on it. But when you've got it, you've got complete control over that horse. But you couldn't hand it over to somebody else. You've got to get your own.

I'm also a big believer in another thing I've got. That is the milt – a lump of flesh like a kidney which, when a foal is born, it spit out 'cos it lay on the tongue to stop the foal swallowing its tongue when it's born. All you need to do is bake the milt and then treat it with various oils. Then, if you've got one of them, there's no horse'll hurt you when you've got that milt in your pocket.

Hector, you're one of the last of the blacksmiths still using your own mixture of aromatic oils to help control or influence horses. How do these oils work?

I wouldn't like to try and explain how these old oils work – but they do. I think probably the biggest factor is that you've got confidence in the oil. So, therefore, all yer fear has gone, you're not worrying, you're calm, you're collected, your actual sweat smell different because, as soon as you start to panic and worry, the scent of your sweat is different, isn't it? Animals can sense that, especially a horse because they rely more on smell than do anything. You can see that by the shape of the nostrils. I mean Nature made them and, of course, they've got two nostrils each side, a horse do.

I think that's how these oils work. With the stronger ones – the ones which are classed as drugs – you have got the doping effect; but not the ordinary, straightforward oils for like catching a horse which you always put on where you sweat. Things of that nature all go back to confidence.

The extraordinary thing about these oils is, until your system get adapted to it, you really feel ill. When you first start using them, they make you feel really ill when you've got them on. But after you've used them and you're adjusted to them you take no notice of them and they don't affect you.

And I think you rub some of these oils on your cap that you always wear. Is that true?

Oh, yes! I wouldn't shoe a horse without my cap. Yes, I like my cap as you can see by the colour of it. Plenty of horses they just take my cap off. They stand there with it in their mouth. That's not a bit unusual.

Is it true that the old horsemen could also use the oils to stop another man's horse moving?

Yes, you can stop a horse. Nobody can move him only that man what put it there. He can do it. I mean a man can stop a horse by putting a chalk mark across the road — mind you, he don't tell you what he soaked the chalk in! A horse can sense smell miles off. And you can use the oils for quieting it, making it frisky. If you want to get your own back on somebody, you can go and make that horse so that man won't be able to do nothin' with it.

So you discovered the secrets of these oils from the old horsemen you spoke to in the pub when you were a young lad?

Oh, yes! As soon as these horsemen realised that you was capable and that you was dedicated to your job and nothing else, they would tell you; but, I mean, that was a struggle to get there. And you'd got to prove yourself. Probably these old men'd think back years, d'you see, and say, 'Well, he's bin a good old boy. He knows what he's a-doing. We'll help him.'

So over the years, you just gained their confidence because they knew that you was dedicated, knew what you were doing. So they would help you. But if you didn't, you wouldn't get it out of them at all. Of course, they told you in confidence. If somebody told you somethin' and that got out that you'd told somebody else, that'd be that! You'd never get nothing else out of 'em. Never!

So what are these oils and where were they obtained?

They're made of various things. The majority of them are herbal oils. And you buy various ones, though you can't get them from a chemist now, unless you're fortunate and know a real old one and then you can get some off the shelf. A few more years and that'll be completely gone.

Now the old horsemen, they'd never get them all from one chemist's shop. No! That was in case that got out how that was mixed, you see. It's the proportions that count. They knew all the stuff, but some had got it down to a very fine art – got it just spot on. They'd always mix their own and, of course, these old horsemen were getting nothin' in wages. Before my time, I've heard these old horsemen talk about twelve shillings a week. But they'd still go to the chemists and buy these oils with their own money. They'd never go and ask the master for any. They'd never let him buy any. It all came out of their own pocket. And they'd go without food on the table to do it.

So they done their upmost to keep their secrets, because they were guarding theirself against being out of a job. If you was a good horseman, you was king o' the farm and you'd got to be better than the man next door or you wouldn't have the job. And if you didn't have the job, you couldn't go on the dole then. So there was always somebody waiting for your job.

* * *

For the cost of quite a few pints of beer, I did manage to obtain some information about some of the oils the old horsemen used.

Of course, I cannot guarantee their efficacy or their accuracy. They are included here only for interest. Obviously, I have never tried to buy them and, indeed, many of the ingredients are now all but unobtainable. So they are included here with the warning: DO NOT USE THEM ON A HORSE or, of course, on your parents, wife, husband or children!

MAIN INGREDIENTS

1) Oil of cumin (from the aromatic seeds of Cuminum cymiinum)
2) Attar (or otto) of roses.
3) Essence of new-mown hay
4) Essence of heliotrope (from Heliotropium arborescence)
5) Tincture of opium (or laudanum)
6) Oil of cinnamon (from the inner bark of Cinnamomum zeylanicum)
7) Oil of fennel (from Foeniculum vulgare)
8) Oil of rosemary (from the leaves of Rosemarinus officinalis)
9) Oil of pennyroyal (from Mentha pulegium – a kind of mint
10) Oil of rhodium (from the scented wood of Canary convolvulus)
11) Oil of origanum (wild marjoram)

RECIPES FOR DEALING WITH HORSES

1) For catching difficult horses
    Bake 1lb of wheat flower, mixed with treacle, into small cakes.

Then rub in your sweat and add 5 drops each of oil of origanum, oil of fennel, oil of rosemary and oil of cinnamon. Feed cake to horse.

2) *For making restive horses stand still (for shows or selling)*
   Rub tincture of opium on head.
3) *For jading (stopping) a horse*
   Rub gate or manger etc. with skin of a dead mole.
4) *For calming horses*
   Add to ¼ ounce of orris powder, 10 drops of oil of origanum and 15 drops each of oil of cumin and pennyroyal. Rub on horse.
5) *For calming horses*
   Bake cakes from wheat flower and treacle. Add drops of oil of cumin, attar of roses, essence of heliotrope and oil of rhodium. Feed cakes to horse.
6) *For obtaining attention of a difficult horse*
   Rub into an object or cloth you carry a mixture of oil of rhodium, essence of new-mown hay and attar of roses.

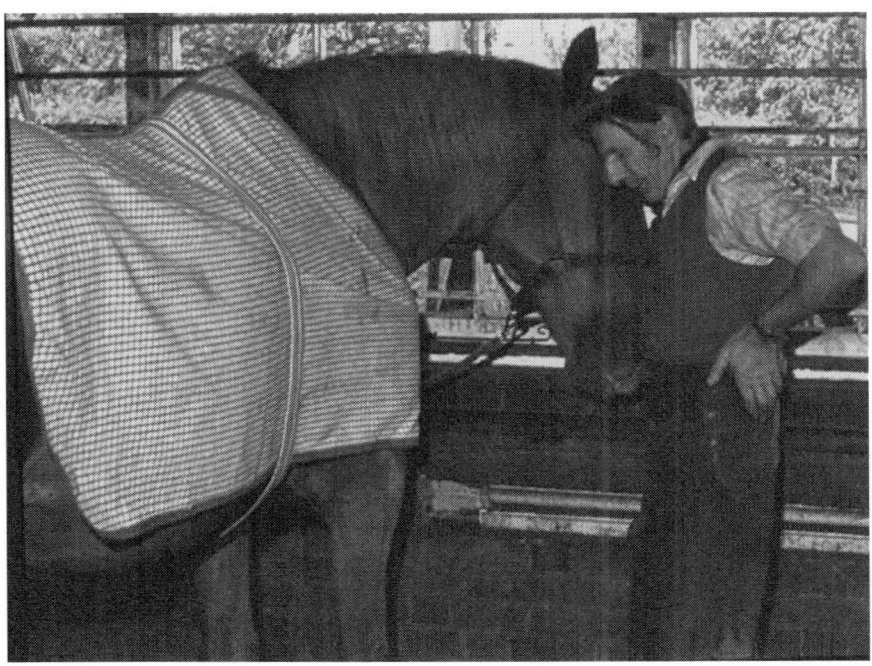

Sydney Higgins

A Traditional Suffolk Folk-Song

THE HORSE PLOUGHMEN

'Twas early one morning at the break of the day.
The young cocks was crowing. The farmer did say,
'Rise up me good fellows and work wi' good will,
for your horses need summat their bellies to fill.'
   Chorus
It's oorily, oorily, oorily, ay!
What have you been doing this long summer's day?
We ain't ploughed an acre, I'll swear and I'll vow.
Oh, you're damned idle fellows as follows the plough.

At four in the morning we rise from our bed,
go down to't pump and we douse on our head.
We curry our horses and tak' 'em in tow
'cause we're damned clever fellows as follows the plough.
   Chorus

At six in the morning, it's breakfast time now.
And welcome it is, I can certainly vow,
with eggs and with bread and a piece of old sow,
'cause we're damned hungry fellows as follows the plough.
   Chorus

We harness our horses, take them to't field
and a plentiful harvest in time we will yield.
We plough all our furrows, all in a straight row
'cause we're damned clever fellows as follows the plough.
   Chorus

And come eventide then our work it shall end.
It's round to the alehouse to toast an old friend.
Put a gallon o' pint pots, all in a straight row,

'cause we're damned thirsty fellows as follows the plough.

Chorus
  It's oorily, oorily, oorily, ay!
  What have you been doing this long summer's day?
  We ain't ploughed an acre, I'll swear and I'll vow.
  Oh, you're damned idle fellows as follows the plough.

Inside Hector Moore's smithy

Farm Labourers

Charlie Fisk – born 1895
Cooker Carver – born 1901
Arthur Boast – born 1920

It was not just the blacksmith with his oils and special frog's bone that believed in magic. So did many of the old horsemen and farm labourers. In most rural areas, the belief was widely held that people and animals could be cursed or evil-wished. When this happened, the curse could be lifted only by the performance of a special ritual. Aware that, in modern times, such practices are likely to be dismissed as being primitive superstitions, many old people are understandably reluctant to talk about their beliefs and experiences. However, while talking to old people, it is sometimes possible to hear unexpected, unsolicited accounts of magical practices and old superstitions.

This happened to me when I was talking to Charlie Fisk, who was then in his early nineties and lived in one of the almshouses in Framlingham. He was a boy before the First World War, and he spoke about his early life and the horsemen he had known.

When I was a boy, my father had three pigs in a sty. One time, two on 'em done well but one wouldn't do. And he said, 'Somebody bewitched that pig. That's what it is.'

He went and cut a load of wood and that night made up a fire indoors. Then he went into the sty, caught the pig, got his knife, cut the pig and drew a little bottle of blood out of it, corked it up and brought it indoors.

Then he says to me, 'Don't you whisper! Don't you say a word!'

He flung the bottle into the middle of the fire and he sat there. I can see him sitting there now, looking at the bottle.

After it began to boil and bubble in the bottle, we heard somebody walking around the house a-calling out most desperate. They was! It's true!

After a bit of that wailing, my mother said, 'Well! You'll have to stop that, dad. I can't put up with it!' Just like that! Well that 'ad broke the spell and, the commotion, it stopped.

Nexter mornin', our next-door neighbour was walking, going to work and got his hand bound up where it'd been burnt. That's the truth! It was him what had bewitched the pig. We all knew that then.

That was a lot of superstitions on the part of Suffolk folks then, you know. Mind, my father was a religious man. He'd never admit he'd done anything wrong. But my Uncle Ted would. He was one of the biggest outers you'd ever see, my Uncle Ted was.

I'll tell you what he done. I know this to be right. He was horseman for the Wilson's at Cretingham and old Mrs Wilson who was down there was always queer.

Old Doctor O'Conner was an Irish doctor down at Earl Soham. Ted was at home there and they said t'im, 'Edgar, will you go and git Dr. O'Conner? The Misses is dying.'

So he said, 'Right!'

He had an old bloody pony that he broke in hisself. Nobody else could drive it. He put it into the cart and went to git Dr O'Conner.

You knows, as you come from Earl Soham towards Cretingham, there's a lot of hills and very sharp corners. He came down one hill and one thing and another and the doctor holding onto the side of the cart. 'D'you know what, Fisk?' he said. 'There ain't only one wheel on the ground when you turned that corner.'

Ted said, 'You're all right. Yow hold tight!'

He took the doctor down to old Mrs Wilson and waited. The doctor gave her something and she got better.

Old Wilson says, 'Edgar, you can take Dr. O'Connor back to Earl Soham.'

Then the doctor said, 'No, Mr Wilson. I won't ride with that mad man no more at all! Tell him to go and get my groom up and he can get my own horse and come and get me.'

And Uncle Ted had to drive there. Well, I'll tell you what he done. All the way there, he cussed Dr. O'Connor for what he'd said.

On the way home, the doctor's wheel came off the cart coming down the hill. It turned over, it did, and he was right shaken. That's what my Uncle Ted done!

Well, I'll tell you, if me Uncle Ted could do anybody down, anything at all, he would.

For years, he rode an old stallion and it was a rum un. Nobody else durst touch it and that's the truth. But it never worried Ted - not one bit. It never hurt him. He used to say, 'I'm his friend. I look after him and he looks after me.'

When he went to the pub, he just used to tie the rein round a stick and throw it on the ground in front of that old horse and it wouldn't move, not till Ted picked up that stick again,

One day, Ted stopped at the Worlingworth *Swan* to have a

bite of cheese and a pint.

This old boy said to Ted, 'Look here, Fisk. Can I pick up that stick and move your horse?'

'Can if you like,' said Ted.

Well everybody went out of the pub to watch and this old boy picks up the stick. Well, that old horse reared up and kicked out and would have done no end of damage if my Uncle Ted hadn't calmed him down and put the stick back on the ground.

'You was lucky!' he said to the old boy. 'If I hadn't been here, it'd have kicked yer bloody skull in.'

You see, my Uncle Ted used to put some special oils on that there stick and while it was there that old horse wouldn't move.

Well later on, my Uncle Ted had a bad accident and he weren't too good after that. So the farmer he worked for told him he weren't to look after the horses no more and he was to be the gardener.

Two young chaps were put to look after the horses. I think they was about seventeen or eighteen and rather thought they knew everything.

The next Monday, they put the horses in the field and, you know, Ted went to the gate, looked over and rubbed his old hand along the top of the gate and walked away.

Well, that evening, those two young chaps couldn't get them horses out. They couldn't get the horses off the meadow. Ted went up there and he said, 'Well, can't you get them off yet? I thought you were horsemen!'

Now Uncle Ted had his boy with him and he was only about eleven or twelve. Ted said to him, 'Look here, boy. Take this here halter and go into the meadow and get them off, boy!'

So his boy went through the gate, went right up to a horse and put the halter ont' it. And they all followed him right out –

about eleven of them. And yet the two lads had been around the meadow there and knocked themselves clean up without one horse moving.

Of course, you know what Uncle Ted had done? He'd put one of his old horsemen remedies on that there gate and those horses couldn't come through till they'd got Ted's scent on that halter! That's what he'd done.

Our family were horsemen all their lives. I loved working with horses but I couldn't always do it. When the slump was, I couldn't get nothin' to do. So I went to Lincolnshire. They paid our fare from Framlingham station to Lincolnshire. It was 17 shillings and 4 pence.

I stopped there two years. I worked on a farm and I should be up there today if it hadn't been for one thing. The folks there got up an outing to Cleethorpes. That particular day, there were two different buses used. I went along with some folks but, coming back, there wasn't room in the first bus and so I had to get in the second.

On the way home, the first bus runned into a bridge and turned over and killed eight folks. I was friendly with an Irish gal up there and she was one of the eight what was killed. I was with her when she died. After that, I couldn't stop up there. So I came on home to Earl Soham. Forty years after, when I was at Saxtead, I got the flu and a strange thing what happened to me. I lived all alone and I wanted a drop to drink but I couldn't go downstairs to get it. And do you know what? As I lay a-bed, there was a hand come from somewhere and give me a drink and d'you know what? It was that there girl that died alongside the road. I'll tell you now how I come to know. I'd given her a ring and it was there on her finger. Now what d'you make of that?

* * *

Still active almost to the end, Charlie Fisk was in his early nineties when he died. He never married.

For much of his working life that lasted for some fifty years,

Charlie looked after the farm animals, especially pigs. When they had been fattened for market, he drove them along the country lanes the four miles from Earl Soham to Framlingham railway station. (It closed for freight trains in 1963.)

He told me that the pigs on the farm were sometimes found to be suffering from syphilis, which he called 'red murrow' because of the reddish-pink rash that is a symptom of the disease. (First used in a poem written in Latin in 1530, the word 'syphilis' is sometimes translated as 'he who liked pigs'.)

In the twentieth century, there were strict regulations in force to ensure that animals found with syphilis should be immediately slaughtered and the corpses should be burnt.

Charlie told me how he was expected to deal with cases of syphilis found among the pigs on the farm where he worked.

It spreads with pigs just like humans really. It starts with a boar who 'as red murrow going to one sow and then another and they catch it and pass it on. Course, you'd got to get rid of 'em.

When any of our pigs got red murrow, I'd work with a bloke what worked in Earl Soham. He was a pig-killer. We'd start perhaps at eight o'clock at night. Perhaps I wouldn't get home much before I'd got to be at work at quarter to seven in the morning. You had to do the work at night 'cause nobody never know what you were about. But there were oft so many pigs with red murrow you'd be killing the things all bloody night.

I used to heat the copper up and boil it so they scolded and then I scraped 'em and all that. Then when they were cleaned up, right early in the mornin', I used to take 'em in the cart to Monewden. There they'd be loaded up and took off to sell in London. Then the people there used to eat the buggers. Of course, you don't know what you're eating even now, d'you?

* * *

Their affinity to the land and their pride in their skill created, in many farmworkers, a fierce independence that outsiders could have seen as stubbornness. Because of these qualities, many labourers insisted - even at the risk of losing their jobs - that they knew better that the farmer how certain tasks should be done. Many also refused to work with a newly hired labourer they thought was incompetent.

Charlie 'Cooker' Carver was such a man.

During the war, I worked for Mr Bloomfield. One day, he went into a field when he was bloody harvestin'. He'd got a field of wheat and d'you know that lay down there as flat as a bloody turd, flat on the ground, all one way. He was a–swearin'.

'Bloody fields,' he say. 'Can't git nothin' done at all.'

He went off to Ashfield or somewhere, saying he was going to set fire to the field.

So I said to his son, 'What's the matter with the old man then about that bloody field of wheat?'

He say, 'It ain't much, Cooker. That's only about two acres on it. But the bloody binder won't cut it!'

I say, 'What d'you mean - the bloody old binder won't cut it? Of course, that'll cut it!'

'D'you think so?'

'Course, it bloody well will,' I say. 'It'll all lay one way. Why don't we take the bloody old binder and cut it?' (He was a young chap, you see.)

He said, 'You ain't goin' to cut it!'

I said, 'I'll cut the bloody thing!'

So we got four or five little lifters and put on the front of the binder. You see, when the bloody corn lay flat all one way, all you do is push it up from the front. You can't go t'other way – over the top of it. That'd just push it down. So I drove the binder up the field, then all the way round, then back up again so we was like cuttin' strips – just one way each time. The boy was drivin' a little old Fordson tractor alongside.

Well Bloomfield comes walkin' into the field and I think we'd cut three-quarters on it. He looked at me sitting on the binder and he say, 'I suppose you think you know more about cuttin' the corn than what I do? Well I've bin a farmer ever since I was a boy!'

I said, 'That's nothin' to do with me, sir, what you think. I'm a-tellin' you I told you we could cut this corn and so we can.'

He said, 'Well all right then, Cooker. Get off!'

I got off the bloody binder and he said to his boy, 'Get on the binder.' The old man took the tractor. And they finished it. He come off the field and he says to me, 'That's finished. You aren't a bad chap at all, you aren't Cooker!'

I said, 'You done that job well. But you done me out of a sitting-down job!'

He cussed at me then but that was just his way. We got on well but then, after the war, an old man came to the farm for a job.

Well Mrs Bloomfield said to me, 'That stupid man's here after a job.'

I said, 'Oh! What do he want to do?'

She said, 'He was yard-man here before the war.'

I said, 'Oh! That's all right then.'

She said, 'But I told my husband we wouldn't have him here!'

She was a nice little lady – nice little woman. I said, 'All right, ma'am.'

She said, 'You like being here, don't you, Cooker?'

I said, 'Course I do, ma'am.' You see I used to do her gardening and cut the bloody old faggots to fill her old brick oven full. It didn't matter what she wanted done, Cooker used to do it. I'd help anybody – still do!

Anyway, I went to work that Sat'day a'ternoon to milk the cows and see 'em loading the bloody man's furniture into the house. So I just went and milked the cows.

Poor little woman, Mrs Bloomfield, came through there crying and said, 'Yew see he's got that man here, don't yew?'

I said, 'Well, I don't know ma'am. I saw the cart unloadin' up there.'

'Yes, that's him' she say. Course, I went to work the Sunday mornin' - the next day. I went in and that bloke was sat there milkin' a cow. I said, 'Mornin'!'

He said, 'Mornin'!'

I said, 'We got a new cowman 'ere?'

'Well,' he said, 'I moved here last night and I'm milkin' this mornin'.'

I said, 'Why the bloody hell didn't you start in Monday mornin' then? What you milkin' the bloody cows for them today?'

'Well,' he said, 'he told me I could startin' milkin' 'em?'

'Oh!' I said. 'That's a rum un!'

He said, 'And he told me you've got twelve calves in the barn.'

I said, 'Yes, there's twelve calves in the barn.' (Course, up to then I used to look after 'em, tie 'em up with halters and give 'em so much milk to rear 'em.)

So he said, 'You've got to stop 'ere and help me finish milkin' these cows.'

I said, 'How many more is there to milk? It looks to me as though you've milked half of 'em. You've got two bloody pails of milk there.'

He said, 'There's that one there for you to milk.'

I said, 'Well, you milk the bugger! I aren't!'

'Well,' he said, 'you've got to help feed the calves.'

'Bugger the bloody calves,' I said, 'and you wi' 'em! Feed 'em yer bloody self!' Course I then turned round and I come out and went home.

Monday mornin', I come back and went through the barn. I said to the bloke, 'Mornin'!'

'Mornin'!' he said. 'We got messed up with 'em calves yesterday.'

'Yes,' I said. 'And you'll get messed up with 'em today.'

'Will I?' he said.

I said, 'Course you bloody-well will, 'cause I'm not goin' to help you do it! Hell! Bugger you and the cows and calves wi' you!'

I went up to the door of the house and Bloomfield come struttin' past me – he was a long tall bugger. And I said, 'Mornin', sir.'

'Haven't got time to talk to you,' he said.

'Why not?' I said. 'You'll have to make time to talk to me, 'cause I want to give you a week's notice from this mornin'. That's about three or four minutes to seven now and I want you to take a week's notice from me today. You can give me a job to do if you like. If not, I'll bloody well go 'ome!'

He wouldn't have me work there! He said, 'Well go down to old Wilson's farm. There's some thatchin' want doin' down there. Will you go and do that, Cooker?'

I said, 'Yes, sir, I'll go.' So I went and got me thatch' things and went down there. I got his beet clamps and finished Johnny Wilson's thatchin'.

The Sat'day mornin', I went up a'ter the money and poor old Mrs Bloomfield was a-cryin' and she said, 'I'm sorry to lose you, Cooker. You're the nicest little lad I've had.'

Poor old woman! But he was a rum old bugger – that he

was.

      But I didn't mind. It didn't matter a piss where I went to. I could go anywhere. I don't care a bugger where they sent me. I don't care what job they gave me. I don't care whether a cow calves, breaks a leg or hangs herself or anythin' else. It wouldn't worry me. I could do the job. There wasn't a job I couldn't do!

* * *

Like many farm labourers, Cooker Carver loved to sing in local pubs. This was one of his favourite songs that he sang for me. It is a good example of the somewhat risqué songs that were extremely popular in the all-male pub society.

A Traditional Suffolk Folk-Song

SWING BOATS

I took me girl out to the fair
to see the sights so grand –
the swinging-boats and shooting stalls
and ev'rything that's grand.
I took her to see the roundabouts.
I took her to see the side-shows.
But the thing that tickled her fancy most
was the swing-boats after all.
  Sarah loved to swing in boats
  She said they were all right.
    I treated her once.
    I treated her twice.
    She did not mind the price.
    For she liked it when it went up high.
    It tickled her when it came back.
    For it made her laugh all over her face
    And half-way down her ... back

And so my money began to fly.
But still I did not care
for I always like to please me gal
when I take her to the fair.
She said, 'Oh, Bill! Oh, ain't this nice?
Let's have another go.'
And every time the boat went up
she never would say no.
  Sarah loved to swing in boats.
She said they were all right.
      I treated her once.
      I treated her twice.
      She did not mind the price.
      For she liked it when it went up high,
      It tickled her when it came back.
      For it made her laugh all over her face
      and half-way down her ... back.

*   *   *

Arthur Boast worked on the same farm continuously for over fifty years. He was a kind, generous and soft-spoken man who took an immense pride in all the work he did on the land that he said he knew as well as the back of his own hand.

When we married, we couldn't get a house in the village. There weren't many houses with this farm. So we had to live in an old house which I'd always looked down on. It was right near the sewage works.

    Well, we had nothing delivered at all – not even the post. We had to go up to the village to me mother's for bread and stuff like that left up at hers. We had to cart the paraffin for the lamps. No television then, of course. We had to get the water out the stream. It was good water – it's still running – but, higher up, about two fields further up, were a herd of cows and, if they took it into their heads to stamp in the stream, then your water was a bit cloudy. And also, if there was a thunder-storm, you had got to look out and get some water in, 'cause otherwise that was thick with mud. We used to carry the water across the field, about a hundred yards – two pails of water at a time.

A lot of people had to do that. They wouldn't waste half as much as they do today because I should say that now there's a lot more water wasted than there is used. And that goes for a lot of other things – not only water. There's a terrific waste of everything and much more untidiness to what there used to be.

Well, we were down there five years. Then we managed to get up to a house where there was electric light and water laid on – and that's where I still am.

The farm has altered quite a bit. There used to be a lot of workmen around here – rather a biggish gang. But things quieted down a bit. The governor gave up one or two farms. As he got older, the family went away and the farm sort of tightened up quite a bit. We started to grow more corn and rather less greens.

As he got older still, madam died. Nice little person – but she died of cancer. He lived on here until he died and then we gave up the farm. I'd helped him run the farm – quite different ideas to what they are today 'cause, for one thing, there was no money. But we were quite happy.

I think, in modern standards, they don't want you to be in one job too long 'cause they think you're not getting on, you're not making any headway. But I don't know – it was thirty-five years I was with him on this farm and it don't seem any amount of time. It don't seem long at all.

After the governor died in 1969, the farm was taken over by the owners of the estate. The governor was only a tenant farmer. I was asked to carry on as a foreman here and quite comfortable it is too. I must say there's no worries like there used to be. When a tractor breaks down now, that's done up properly and I don't have the worry of that. But I used to have the worry of going to the engineers and seeing about having it done up and, of course, cost was one of the biggest things.

You'd say, 'Patch it up!'

They'd say, 'No, bung in a new engine,' like they do today.

And you'd say, 'No!' because it cost too much money. When the repair was finished, you'd take them a sack of potatoes and say, 'That's that!'

There's something about working out in the open-air, out on the land. I couldn't work inside. I remember having the old tractor done up and, while they were repairing the engine and doing it up, I painted it. I was in the garage for a couple of days. Oh dear! That roof over your head all the while, that seemed awful, you know. It seemed a right treat to get out!

You get more satisfaction out of doing ploughing and drilling than any other thing on the farm, I should think. I don't know why, 'cause ploughing is a very monotonous job. You just go backwards and forwards but I'm sure, if you ask any of the tractor drivers or the old horsemen, they always got a satisfaction out of it.

When I was younger, the old horsemen didn't go to church on a Sunday; they'd walk on their own around the fields to cast an eye over to check what had been done. They wanted to see how perfect their furrows were and whether anybody was better than they were!

Now I don't do any ploughing and I don't do any drilling. being the foreman, you just do odd jobs here and there, run here and there, and do this, that and t'other. But you miss the ploughing!

There must be satisfaction and you must like the job. You haven't been doing it for the money. You haven't been working on the land for the money – nobody have!

Most farm workers do like their garden. That's the main thing you'll hear: 'Have you got your onions in?' or 'Have you got a row of new 'tatoes in?' But you've got to work to do that. If you've got a load of wood, you've got to saw it up, you've got to get it home and you've got to saw it up again into lengths when you get there. That's just a way of life, the way of living, the way you're brought up.

When I get home at nights, like last night, I had my tea and I said, 'Well, I'll go and do some work.' Well, they're getting used to hearing me say that. I just go out. Probably I don't know what I'm going to do until I get my coat and hat on and get outside. Then I think, 'Well, I'll do this.' That's just a habit to do something.

What I can't understand is how people can go through life without making something or doing something so that they can see it, see what they've done. That's what I want to do. I want to see what I've done. I want to plant a shrub or something like that. If I had plenty of money and I bought some land, I should plant flowering shrubs all over it. I'm sure I should. I shouldn't be able to resist buying them.

I think routine is one of the biggest things in life. Once you start laying abed and wake up and look at the same time and it's about eleven o'clock or something like that, I don't think you feel any better for it. You don't feel any better for just laying in bed.

I think when I and my family have our little jaw about this, that and t'other, we all agree now that we've altered our way of thinkin' a bit. Years ago, they used to think, 'Well, save! A shilling or two here and a shilling or two there.' Well, we think now that you want to be a bit thrifty – you never know when you might have a bit of bad luck and you want a pound note – but other than that, to scrape and save every penny, I don't think there's much sense in that. I think if you want anything reasonable and you've got the money, buy it because it's later than you think. People keep thinkin' we want so-and-so tomorrow, the next day or somethin' like that. They forget that today is here and you won't get this day back again. So you've got to live this day and enjoy it!

Now I'm sure there are thousands of people who're not really enjoyin' their lives. They get up in just enough time to go to work. They hare off somehow by car or train or somethin'. And if you were to say suddenly to them, 'Are there any leaves on the trees?' they'd have to stop and think whether there were any on the trees or not. They don't notice things as they go about, a lot of people, because they haven't the time. Well, I always say the only time they'll get is when they're in their coffins!

Do you ever wish that you hadn't spent all your life working for someone else?

Oh, no! No, not at all! The old governor would have told you that I've always treated the farm as mine. I'd probably worry as much as he did about a crop that was going wrong or a tractor that broke down. I know he'd got to pay for it but it didn't make any difference. I've always treated the things as my own. I still do.

I remember, a few years back, a keeper on a large estate told me, 'This estate belongs to me.'

And I said, 'Oh, how d'you make that out?'

'Well,' he said, 'it do. I can walk all over the estate, all through the woods and meadows and everywhere. And I enjoy the estate a lot more that the governor do. Therefore, it's my estate,'

And he was right. Because, never mind whether that's on a bit of paper that belongs to somebody, he was enjoying it a lot more than the owner was. So if there's anything on that field and it look nice, well I enjoy it. I enjoy seeing it grow. You can't help it.

A Traditional Suffolk Folk-Song
BUTTERCUP JOE

(There are hundreds of versions of this traditional song. I recorded this one in the Worlingworth Swan.*)*

Now I be a true-bred country chap.
Me father comes from Fareham.
Me mother's got seven more like I
and she well knows how to rear 'em.
Some people calls I 'bacon fat'
and others, 'turnip head'.
But I can prove I ain't no flat
though I be country bred.
    Chorus
      For I can plough or milk a cow.
      I can reap or sow.
      I be fresh as a daisy bloomin' in the fields.
      And they calls I 'Buttercup Joe'.

Now have you seen my pretty maid?
They call her Little Mary.
She works as busy as a bumblebee,
down In Sir Johnstone's Dairy.
And dun't she make those dumplings nice?
Full well I mean to try 'em.
For next to them she'd love to 'ave
a country chap like I am.
    Chorus

Some people they likes hay makin'
and others they like mowin'.
But the job of all that I like best
is a job called sugar-beet hoein'.
So when I weds my Little Mary
and takes her to me bed,
I'll always keep her dumplins warm
although I'm country-bred.
Chorus
    For I can plough or milk a cow.
    I can reap or sow.
    I be fresh as a daisy bloomin' in the fields.
    And they calls I 'Buttercup Joe'.

The Servants

Kate Middleditch – born 1905
Ivy Burrell – born 1902

Many Suffolk villages during the first half of the Twentieth Century were dominated by a large landowner or squire whose imposing residence was staffed by the daughters and sons of impoverished tenants. However, even in such closed or feudal villagers, the number of servants recruited annually by the squire and his wife was very small. Village girls entering service were more likely to be employed in the towns by local traders and businessmen who, until the outbreak of the Second World War, expected to have at least a couple of servants.

It is easy to understand why so many young people from country villages were happy to enter into service. At home, there was a large family and poverty. Breakfast might well be nothing more than a slice of raw turnip. For them, the evening meal was often nothing more than pieces of stale bread soaked in the water in which the vegetables had been cooked - the limited amount of vegetables being the meal of the workingman of the household. In great contrast, servants, even though they might receive a minimal wage, would normally enjoy the luxury of sleeping in their own bed and being adequately fed.

Kate Middleditch, unlike most young women in service, worked in several establishments before she left work to get married. (It was not only the normal practice for married women not to work, it was, in many occupations, illegal. For example, it was not until 1944 that married women were allowed to teach in the UK.)

When I spoke to Kate, she was a widow in her mid-seventies who still recalled with some bitterness that, during her years spent as a servant, she was treated as an inferior not only by her employers but also by the other, more senior servants.

As soon as I left school, my mother said one of us had got to get out. She wanted the bed space. You see, there were eleven of us children at home and I was in the middle. My mother heard that the Pauls of Orwell Lodge, Ipswich, needed a scullery maid. So she fixed it up and, that September, I went there. I was fourteen.

When I went there, I had a new pair of flat shoes that cost about ten bob. I had three print dresses, four big white aprons and four mop-caps. Then I had nighties and that kind of thing. I think my mother spent about twelve pounds on my uniform.

Well I'd got a long pigtail down my back. Of course, as soon as Mrs Paul saw that, it had to be pinned up under my cap. No hair down your back you weren't allowed to have. That was the rules. So my long pigtail that everybody used to admire had to be pinned up and put under my cap to cover as much as possible.

There was the kitchen maid and me in two single beds in one room and in the next bedroom was two of the housemaids. Being the scullery maid, I was the lowest – the bottom rung of the ladder.

We used to get up at six and the housemaid used to come through and do my hair up 'cause I couldn't manage it. We washed in a basin and jug in the bedroom. They were in a wash-hand stand. So one of us had to get up a little before the other to get washed. Of course, we didn't have hot water. It was cold water. And there was no heating in the bedrooms – nothing. Then I'd put on my uniform.

We'd go downstairs about half past six and I'd go to the scullery. Now my first job was to scrub with a hearthstone the big front step that was almost as big as a rug. It used to be done over sort of grey. Then there were two scrapers either side that they used to scrape their boots on and I had to black-lead them. You see, the chauffeurs when they used to come to pick somebody up used to put their shoes on them to clean them before they came into the main hall.

Now I'd been there a week. Mrs Paul used to come down and give the cook her orders at ten in the morning. Now I was never allowed to be in the kitchen. So I never saw what went on. I had to come through the kitchen but I was never allowed to stay in there.

So, of course, I was in the scullery that day when Mrs Paul came down and I heard her say, 'She'll have to be shown to do it properly.'

I thought, 'Hello! I haven't done it right!' So that morning, the kitchen maid had to show me how the step should be scrubbed properly. See, you weren't allowed to leave any marks.

After cleaning the step, I used to clear up the scullery and get the plates ready for breakfast. There was nothin' in the scullery, only cobble stones and a big copper in the corner – I can see it now – and a great big sink. We used to heat the water for washing up in the copper. There was no tap water in those days. And that scullery weren't no bigger than a tiny kitchen in the house and I lived in there, apart from my meals. I was in there practically from morn till night when I went to bed.

All the rough work was done in there – the pluckin' of the pheasants and the skinning of the rabbits and the cutting 'em up. So, of course, during the shooting season, they'd take the game down into the cellar and they used to be brought to me all green. They never ate them till they were green. And I used to have to pluck them and draw them. I've done as many as six in a day when we had the dinner parties.

At seven-thirty, we used to go into the staff dining room, where we all sat together – except the butler. He never came in and had a meal with us – nor did the cook. She used to be preparing the meal. She had hers when she wanted it, 'cause she was elderly. She was a marvellous cook. But they never let me see anything. That's what I was interested in – cooking – but I never did learn anything about it there.

But we ate quite well. At breakfast, we all had a half-pound of farm butter on our plates round the table with our names on. That had to last for the week. If you used it up before the end of the week, well then you had to go without. We used to have porridge and a cereal and, occasionally, we'd have a rasher of bacon and a piece of fried tomato. There was always marmalade on the table. Yes, we ate quite well but, being young, there probably wasn't quite enough for me.

Now, at a quarter to nine, I used to have to put on a clean white apron and we used to go into mornin' prayers. At nine o'clock, they were. I used to have to be last because I was scullery maid. The cook never went in and the butler never went in, nor the lady's maid – well, we hardly ever saw her. So there were five of us at prayers: three housemaids – that was head housemaid, second housemaid and third housemaid – then the kitchen maid and me, the scullery maid. Mr. Coleman, the butler, used to stand in the pantry and laugh as we'd go through to mornin' prayers.

Mr. Paul used to sit at the head of the long table and Mrs William Paul used to sit on his left. The other chairs were turned outwards from the table so we could kneel at them – we weren't allowed to sit on 'em! Of course, I used to be last in but, instead of coming out first, I had to stand there and let the others go before me. I was always last and it used to annoy me. We went to prayers every day, seven days a week.

After the prayers, I used to be in the scullery and I never came out of there until lunchtime. I just had to prepare the game according to the orders what the cook had and then all the plates. I never touched no glassware or silver or went in the pantry. The butler did all that. I used to be allowed to take the plates into the kitchen 'cause there was a big double range there and the plates were always kept on the top so they were always nice and hot. I'd have all the staff crockery to do and the plates and the dishes for the dining room. And, of course, all the cooking utensils I had to do – and those kind of people use a lot of utensils! They didn't think about how many saucepans and things were used! So I'd have a lot to do. I'd have to wash and clean all those heavy things – big saucepans. Nearly killed me!

Lunch was at one o'clock and we had that in the staff dining room. The cook used to do our cooking and the kitchen maid used to take everything into there. She'd also do some of the cooking for the staff – like the vegetables and that. There was always a stockpot on the range. That was only occasionally cleaned and a fresh lot made. They never made anything with gravy. It was always from the stockpot.

About half past two, when I had washed up and scrubbed all the cobbled floor of the scullery. I'd go up to the bedroom and have a good wash. In the winter, I could take a jug of hot water up with me. Then, after about a half hour's rest, I come down into the scullery again and started getting ready for the evening meal. There was always washing up! I used to stand at the sink for hours and hours. That's why they say I became flat-footed – with the standing so long on the cobbles.

Tea was at half past four. The cook used to make a great big cake in the tin once a week and it used to be cut into squares. So we always had a bit of cake.

In my scullery, there was a little window to the outside and I used to watch the cars draw up. When the guests used to come to dinner parties – on summer nights, the light nights – I used to love to watch at the window to see them all arrive. That was the only part I really enjoyed. They had marvelous dinner parties.

Once I said to Mr Coleman, the butler, I would like to see the table when it was set.

'You shall,' he said. 'I'll show you the table.' So he took me in the dining room and they had all their own crested china and the silverware. It was marvellous really.

Outside the scullery was a great big place where they kept all the fruit from the gardens, 'cause there were three gardeners there and two chauffeurs. All the fruit was laid out in straw. When the butler went through to get the fruit for dinner, the kitchen maid and I often used to pinch a pear or an apple. We'd hide it behind the copper until the butler had gone. That was the only time we got any fruit. But, when the plates used to come through from the dinner parties, there used to be quite a feed left on them. And the kitchen maid used to come through into the scullery with me and we'd have quite a feast off the plates.

At night, we finished at ten. You see, dinner wasn't until a quarter past eight. By the time they'd finished and I'd got my crocks through to wash, it was getting on. And you were never allowed to leave anything. It all had to be clear to start the next morning.

I used to have to go to the farm every Tuesday morning. Well, the first week I was there, the kitchen maid took me with the basket to bring the butter back. The next week, I had to go alone. I went right round the garden and down towards the farm. Course, there were some cows there and I dare not pass. So I came back without the butter but the cook made me turn round and go right back again.

I had a half a day a week off on a Tuesday. I used to come out of the house about three and I had to be back in at half-past nine sharp. Course, you always had to come round the back way. You were never allowed to use the front entrance ever. And they always wanted to know where you went. You had to tell them. Mrs

Paul would ask.

Then, I'd have Sunday morning off one week and, the next Sunday, a half-day. Well, each Sunday morning, I had to go to chapel. I went to one in Tacket Street, about three miles away, where the Pauls went. They'd pass me in their cars but I had to walk.

And I didn't have any holidays. Well, twice I was given a weekend off from the Friday evening to the Sunday evening.

And my money! I started off with a pound a month. They said my mother had started me out so well in uniform that, when I took my first month's money, the cook said to me, 'What you doing with it?' And, she told me, I'd got to give my mother half for buying all my clothes. So ten shillings was taken out of my money each month and I had ten shillings to last me the month. With that, I used to mainly buy a few sweets, which I kept in a drawer in my bedroom.

Course, I used to weep a lot in them days. It was hard, heavy work. And most of the time I was on my own. There was an old parrot in the kitchen and sometimes, when cook was out, I used to go and sit in the kitchen and talk to the parrot for a couple of minutes – but I wasn't really allowed in the kitchen.

I only stuck it at the Pauls' for a year. My father could see me going downhill. I was all pale and thin. So, one Sunday when I went home, my father said I'd got to come away from there. See my mother wanted me to stay but my father said I was to leave.

The next day, I said to the cook I wanted to leave.

'Oh, but you can't!' she said.

I said, 'My father says I've got to.'

She said, 'Well what d'you think you're goin' to do?'

I said, 'I'm going to get a job as a between maid.'

She didn't like it, of course, but I left. The Pauls never said nothin'. They probably didn't even know I'd gone. They just don't want to know.

While she was working as a between maid for a year or so, Kate Middleditch learnt quite a lot about cooking and then, at the age of seventeen, she obtained a position as the cook in a large farmhouse in Grundisburgh.

I lived there very well 'cause I did all the cooking. I was in the kitchen all the time and I was responsible. We had a kitchen boy what did the rough work. He used to bring the milk in and I'd skim the cream off and put it in a container. Then, once a week, I used to make the butter.

I used to make all the bread and every time I used to make an extra loaf and take it home to me mother – she'd still got three at school and me father was ill.

There was a gre't big range and I made all the lovely cakes and stuff. I cooked all the meals and they had lots of dinner parties. Course, in them days they had good plain food. They didn't have all the bits and pieces like they do today. But I'd do the stuffed olives and the soup and all that. Course, they had the poultry yard and there was plenty of eggs and plenty of butter. I cooked everything in butter – all the cakes and everything.

By that time, I was courting and he used to cycle over there when they were out. When I knew I'd be on my own, I used to send him a telegram – used to cost me a bob! He used to come into the dairy and help me there. We made the butter in a big wooden churn and you had to turn it with a big handle. So he was very handy.

Well once he came over and he got caught. They were going to dinner at a house in Framlingham but they didn't get through 'cause of the floods. Of course, they came back and found him there. That tore it! They said he'd no business there. Well I was eighteen then and I felt I could stand on my own two feet and say what I felt like. So I left and applied for another job.

Over the next five years, Kate worked for a number of people.

Immediately before her marriage, at the age of twenty-three, she was employed for three months by a Free Church minister.

That was the miserablist house I'd ever worked in. They were so mean. That Christmas I spent there, I'll never forget the stuff that came into that house. I did nothin' for about a fortnight but answer the door and take in parcels upon parcels. The stuff they had given them! They didn't have to go out and buy food for months. There were tins of biscuits and tins of sweets. There was hams. There was chickens. There was braces of pheasant. There was everything! It all poured into that place!

Of course, it was all put in the pantry and that was always kept locked. Everything was under lock and key. When I did the cooking, I had to ask for everything and then she used to weigh it up for me!

A Traditional Suffolk Folk-Song

A GREASY COOK

I fell in love wi' a greasy cook
  and that I can't deny.
I fell in love wi' a greasy cook
  and here's the reason why.
Yes, and here's the reason why.

Plum puddin', roast beef a-plenty,
  plum puddin' and roast beef,
And when me belly is empty,
  boy, she'd give to me relief.
Yes, she'd give to me relief.

I kindly was invited
  all for supper to take.

And kindly did I accept it
  all for me old belly's sake.
Yes, for me old belly's sake.

Now after the supper was over
  to the larder she got the keys.
One pocket she crammed with butter,
  the other she crammed with cheese.
Yes, the other she crammed with cheese.

Her master a-smelling of the cheese
  let out such a might bawl.
With nowhere to hide me face,
  I up the chimney did crawl
Yes, up the chimney did crawl.

I hadn't been up there very long,
  all a-sitting at me ease,
when the fire it melt me butter
  and also toast me cheese.
Yes, and also toast me cheese.

Each drop that fell into the fire,
  it caused the fire to spit.
Th'old woman said it was the end.
  The devil was a-doin' it.
Yes, the devil was a doin' it.

Her master climbed to the chimney top
  and a pail of water he let fall
and I came tumbin' after
  with me butter, cheese and all.
Yes, with me butter, cheese and all.

The dogs they barked, the children screamed.
  Up flew th'old windows tall.

>Th'old woman cried out, 'Well done! Well done!
>There goes our butter, cheese and all!
>There's our butter, cheese and all!'

* * *

Unlike Kate Middleditch, there were servants who readily accepted their position and enjoyed working for the gentry. One such was Ivy Burrell who trained as a dressmaker and, when she was twenty-one, became one of the lady's maids at Parham Hall.

Parham Hall, Suffolk, 1810

She left there eight years later to marry Billy Wright a most gentle man and an expert carpenter who spent much of his life restoring antiques and expertly crafting perfect copies of them. They were a delightful couple who were both in their eighties when I spoke to them in their small apartment at the back of his large and very cluttered workshop in Framlingham.

As was always the case, Ivy did most of the talking.

I went to an agency in town and saw where these ladies advertised for servants. At Parham Hall, they wanted a lady's maid, cum sewing maid. So I write to her and she sent a letter saying she would like for me to go but did I know my manners, such as opening the door for her to go out and several things like that such as calling her 'Madam'.

Anyway, I went. Course, I was absolutely shy those days and I was right glad she didn't want me to do her hair 'cause I'd had no experience in doing hair. But hers was short and she did her own or went to a hairdresser's in London. But there was plenty to do. It took all my time looking after her and, when her daughter finished at school, I had the two of them. And you know what a young girl of eighteen would be like!

I had my own bedroom and I'd get up about seven. We'd have breakfast at eight, 'cause there was a big staff there then at Parham Hall. There were eight others – parlour maid, under parlour maid, housemaid, under housemaid, kitchen maid, scullery maid, cook and then the housekeeper. The housekeeper was in charge and then I came next, 'cept I was on my own – nobody worked for me.

After breakfast, I'd go and polish up what I wanted and then I had to take her breakfast up because she was more or less an invalid or 'delicate' shall we say. I did that at nine. The cook prepared it and I had to go down to the kitchen, get it on a tray and take it up to her bedroom.

Then she'd have her bath. Sometimes I'd run it and sometimes she'd do it herself. She'd be a long time in the bath and I'd have to put her things out – her clothes what I thought she was going to wear, although sometimes she'd say, 'I'll have my red dress' or 'I'll have my black'. Then I'd get everything out to match – shoes, the right colour stockings and beads – all things like that. Then I'd help her dress when she came out of the bathroom.

After that, she'd mess about. She wouldn't go down till lunch at nearly one. But I'd go to the sewing room and work, making things like dressing gowns, dressing jackets, nighties and sometimes dresses – only plain ones 'cause she used to buy most of her dresses, though she'd always want them altered. She used to buy a lot 'cause I didn't have the time to do a lot of sewing. There was a lot to be done. I had to do all the washing, mending and ironing – for her and her daughter.

We had lunch at twelve o'clock and tea about half past four. I'd finish work about six o'clock. But I always used to sit in the sewing room and do my own sewing or write letters. I very rarely went down into the staff room – very seldom. I preferred to be on my own.

I had a half-day a week off and the morning or afternoon off every other Sunday. But, if she was going out paying calls, even on a Sunday, I had to wait there and get her things out, put the cards in her bag and her gloves and all this and the other. Perhaps it was half-past three or four o'clock before I got off. I don't call that a half-day! But I had a fortnight a year holidays and I was very lucky 'cause she gave me Christmas Day off and so I was always home for Christmas.

We used to go to dances, us girls, and I used to go when I'd finished work – when the beds were turned down and I'd put her night things out. Then she said, 'You can go, Burrell.' (They used to call me by my surname - the senior servants by their surnames and under-ones by their Christian names).

Well, it was often ten o'clock by the time we got down to these dances. They were held in the village halls round about and we girls used to cycle there. One day on my half-day off, we started about six o'clock to get to the dance and we had long frocks on then. It was pouring with rain and we pinned our dresses up round our waists but we were sodden when we got there. These village halls had those pot-bellied stoves with a chimney right up to the ceiling. We stood round that and well you can imagine! All the steam was a-coming off us. Oh dear!

Then it got I was so tired after the dance that I couldn't do all my work. I couldn't stand the late nights, you see. But she put a stop to that and so, when I went to a dance, I had to go to bed for an hour in the afternoon. She made me do that.

I met Billy at a dance. He played the drums in a band. We were courting for eight years before we got married.

Billy: Oh, yes! She tried to push me into it but I weren't havin' any!

Ivy: We used to meet when I had time off and some nights he'd come over and I'd slip out the backdoor in what we called the boot-hole where the chauffeur used to clean the men's shoes. That was right next to the kitchen and it was lovely and hot. Then sometimes if I had to pop upstairs he'd go into the servants' hall with the other girls and chase them around! I suppose it took so long before we married because neither of us were in the mood.

Billy: Well, there weren't many houses to be had, was there?

Ivy: He was a funny fellow to court. He wouldn't kiss you goodnight very often. He'd just say, 'Good afternoon!'

Billy: Plenty good enough!

Ivy: You were a rum boy, weren't you?

Billy: No different to what a lot of others were, I suppose.

Ivy: Anyways, after ten years there, I left to get married. I enjoyed the work and I liked being there. Mind you, I had to work hard but I've always had to work hard in my time – I have since.

But they were nice people to work for. Even after I was married, I went there two half days a week to still carry on doing her sewing and that – not to wait on her 'cause I wasn't there to wait on her, but to do her sewing. I'd bring it home and do it.

I did that for several years until she died. I went on a Tuesday and fitted her for a dress and on Wednesday she took the train to London. There, at Liverpool Street station, she got into a taxi and died. It was a blow.

Although, the death had happened more than fifty years earlier, Ivy was obviously upset by the memory. She said she'd make us all a cup of tea and went to the kitchen. When she returned, with a tray laden with china cups and plates of scones and cup-cakes, it was clear that her normal cheerful mood had returned.

We chatted about things for a while and then returned to her experiences as a lady's maid. After a while, I asked a question:

Ivy, I've spoken to a lot of people who, like you, were in service. Many of them disliked the experience. You obviously didn't.

No. I loved all my time at Parham Hall.

But there must have been something you didn't like - something you didn't like doing. For example, you said you were pleased you didn't have to look after your mistress's hair.

Well, I suppose there was the shoes!

You mean you didn't like cleaning her shoes?

It wasn't that I minded cleaning shoes. But they were green.

I'm sorry. I don't understand.

Well, they were green.

What don't like you like about green shoes, Ivy?

It wasn't that they were really green. They went green.

Why?

You know!

I'm afraid I don't know, Ivy.

You do know!

I'm sorry I don't, Ivy.

Well, it was the way they went green!

Sorry. I still don't understand.

Well, it was what happened then. When you were out, there was no toilets then. You see, the women wore long dresses. When they had to go, they just peed in the streets - and that pee made the shoes turn green. Didn't matter if they were black or blue. They turned green.

Now I understand!

So now you see why me cleaning them shoes wasn't a job I was happy doing!

* * *

In Mrs Beeton's 'The Book of Household Management' (1861), are listed the 'Duties of the Lady's-Maid'. It includes instructions on cleaning the lady's shoes:

'The *Chausserie*, or footgear of a lady, is one of the few things left to mark her station and requires special care. Satin boots or shoes should be dusted with a soft brush, or wiped with a cloth. Kid or varnished leather should have the mud wiped off with a sponge charged with milk, which preserves its softness and polish. The following is also an excellent polish for applying to ladies' boots, instead of blacking them: mix equal proportions of sweet-oil, vinegar, and treacle, with 1 oz. of lamp-black. When all the ingredients are thoroughly incorporated, rub the mixture on the boots with the palm of the hand, and put them in a cool place to dry. Ladies' blacking, which may be purchased in 6d, and 1s. bottles, is also very much used for patent leather and kid boots, particularly when they are a little worn. This blacking is merely applied with a piece of sponge, and the boots should not be put on until the blacking is dry und hardened.'

If this was still the practice when Ivy was a lady's maid, it isn't surprising she would have objected, under the circumstances she recalls, to rubbing 'the mixture on the boots with the palm of the hand'!

Suffolk Farmhouse Recipes

Up until till the 1950s, the families of may Suffolk farm labourers had barely sufficient to eat. With little money and often no cooking facilities other than a small open fire, they ate what they managed to obtain and survived as best they could.

It was in the kitchen of the farmers and tradesmen where interesting, appetizing fare was prepared, as often as not by a cook and her assistants rather than by the lady of the house. It is then from such Suffolk farm homes and the people who worked in them that I have collected these recipes of 'good plain food', made from ingredients that were once more readily available than they may be now.

RABBIT AND HARE

PREPARING THE RABBIT

Cutting
1.　This should be done as soon as possible. (Some hunters gut

the rabbit immediately after it has been killed.) Cover a table with newspaper and use a very sharp knife.
2. Lay the rabbit on the table, head towards you, and insert knife just below breastbone. Make one cut, parallel to the backbone, to the base of the tail.
3. Pick the rabbit up with fore legs in one hand and hind legs in the other. Turn over and empty intestines onto the newspaper. Then feel inside to ensure all the organs have been removed.
4. Keep the liver and kidneys. Throw away the rest.

Skinning
1. Cut off the fore and hind legs at the first joint.
2. Detach skin from flesh and pull over the hind legs.
3. Pull skin over the back and slip out the fore legs. Ease over the head with a knife, if necessary. (If difficulties arise, make a cut through the skin across the back and then remove skin by pulling off both ways.) Alternatively, if head is not required, the neck can be cut through and the head and the complete skin separated from the body.

Cleaning
1. Make a slit between hind legs and wash out with cold water.
2. Remove heart and lungs by cutting the membrane enclosing them inside the rib cage.
3. Wash rabbit thoroughly under cold running water.
4. Before cooking, it is best to soak the rabbit for about an hour in salt water.

Jointing
1. Cut the hind legs off at the backbone.
2. Cut the backbone at the start of the ribs. (This joint is called 'the saddle'.)
3. Divide the fore part of the rabbit down the backbone into 2 joints, each with a fore leg and half the ribcage.

RABBIT PIE

1 rabbit
225 gr./8 ounce belly pork
2 onions
salt and pepper
25 gr./1 ounce flour
bay-leaf and a little sage
300 ml./½ pint stock from the rabbit bones
   For the suet crust pastry:
350 gr./12 ounce self-raising flour
175 gr./6 ounce shredded suet
salt and pepper

1. Having prepared the rabbit, boned and cut it into portions, put meat into soak for 1 hour.
2. Meanwhile, put into a pan the rabbit bones, one of the onions chopped and salt and pepper to taste. Cover with water, boil and simmer for 1 hour.
3. Drain the rabbit portions and dry with a cloth.
4. Transfer the rabbit portions, the bayleaf, sage, the chopped second onion and the stock to a pie dish.
5. For the pastry, mix the flour, suet, salt and pepper. Add sufficient cold water to make flexible dough that does not stick to the mixing bowl.
6. Roll the pastry out in a circle that is a larger than the pie dish. Cut a strip off from the edge of the circle. Press this strip around the top of the dish. Place the circle of pastry over the meat. Decorate as you wish but leave a small hole to allow steam to escape. Bake for 30 minutes or until the top has turned a light brown.

RABBIT CASSEROLE

1 rabbit cut into pieces
1 small cabbage
450 gm./1lb. of small sausages
4 rashers of bacon

1 small onion
150 ml./¼ pint stock
300 ml./½ pint dry cider
bay-leaf and a little sage
salt and pepper

1. Slice the cabbage and boil for 5 minutes in a little water and then drain well.
2. Peel and slice the onion and fry with the sausages until the sausages are brown.
3. In a large casserole dish, put the drained cabbage, rabbit, sausage, onions and uncooked bacon.
4. Cover with the stock and cider.
5. Add the mixed herbs and seasoning.
4. Cover well and simmer for around 2½ hours in a slow oven.

GAME

Pheasants are usually hung for seven to ten days. They are then plucked, dawn and either boned or trussed for eating. Pigeons are better drawn as soon as possible after killing. Snipe, plovers, quails and woodcock are plucked before eating but not drawn.

PIGEON CASSEROLE

4 pigeons
25 gr./1 ounce butter
50 gr./2 ounce belly pork
25 gr./1 ounce plain flower
300 ml./½ pint cider
300 ml./½ pint chicken stock
225 gr./8 ounce onions, cubed
salt and pepper

1. Truss pigeons.
2. Melt butter in a frying pan and fry the finely sliced pork until golden. Place pork slices into the casserole.

3. Fry pigeons in the butter until well browned and then add pigeons to the pork in the casserole.
4. Fry onions in the butter and, as they start to brown, sprinkle in the flour. When both are brown add to the casserole.
5. Pour the hot stock over the pigeons. Season.
6. Cover and cook in a pre-heated moderate oven (Gas 3 or 325°) until tender (about 2½ hours).
7. Add the cider and simmer for a further 10 minutes.
8. Serve with forcemeat balls fried in butter.

Forcemeat balls
    50 gr./2 ounce suet
    100 gr./4 ounce breadcrumbs
    50 gr./2 ounce small pieces of dry cured bacon
    1 small lemon (zest and juice)
    1 large egg (beaten)
    chopped fresh parsley

1. Stir together the suet and breadcrumbs. Then, stir in the chopped bacon. Next, stir in fresh parsley to fleck the mixture evenly. Finally, stir in the lemon zest and then the juice.
2. Add the beaten egg and mix thoroughly.
3. Form mixture into 6 to 8 balls.
4. Put each ball on a greased shallow baking tin and flatten slightly.
5. Bake for 30 minutes, turning once after 15 minutes.

PIGEON PIE

    4 pigeons
    400 gm./1 lb. rump (or lean shoulder) steak
    100 gm./4 ounce ham
    300 ml./½ pint stock
    100 gm./4 ounce mushrooms
        or 2 hardboiled eggs
    salt and pepper
    puff or shortcrust pastry
    yoke of 1 egg

1. Cut each pigeon into 4 pieces. Cut the steak into thin slices, the ham into strips and the mushrooms (or boiled eggs) into slices.
2. Into a pie-dish, put in layers the steak, the pigeon pieces and the ham. Cover with mushrooms (or eggs) and season. Add stock.
3. Put on a lid of pastry and brush over with the beaten yoke of egg.
4. Bake in a pre-heated oven (Gas 7 or 425°) for 30 minutes. Then reduce temperature (to Gas 5 of 350°) for 1 hour.
5. Serve either hot or cold.

GIBLET PIE

The giblets of a goose or duck
2 onions, finely chopped
salt and pepper
400 gr./1 lb. apples
puff or flaky pastry
450 ml./¾ pint stock

1. *Prepare the giblets*

    Throw the head away. Wash the giblets several times in lukewarm water. Then remove the gall from the liver; skin the gizzard and but into halves along the pipe that leads from one end to the other; skin the neck and divide into three pieces; and cut the heart and liver into halves. Put the legs and claws into boiling water to loosen the skin that should then be removed.
2. Put giblets into a saucepan, cover with cold water and then boil. Drain giblets and throw the water away.
3. Pour fresh water on the giblets and add the onions and seasoning. Stew gently until the meat is tender (about 1½ hours). It may be necessary for the feet and gizzard to stew a little longer than the other giblets.
4. Leave the giblets in the water over night.
5. Peel, core and slice the apples.

6. Place in a pie dish alternate layers of giblets and apples. Pour on stock and add necessary seasoning.
7. Put on a lid of pastry.
8. Bake slowly (Gas 3 or 325°) for about 1½ hours).
9. Serve either hot or cold.

PORK

Up until the nineteen twenties, if meat was eaten by richer Suffolk families, it was much more likely to be pork or bacon rather than beef or mutton. Almost all farmers and many labourers kept their own pigs that were usually slaughtered in the autumn so that the hams could be eaten at Christmas.

CURING HAMS

The method of curing hams seems to have been unique to Suffolk. My informant was Mrs Ashwell (known to many as 'Granny Mill' because her husband, before his death, had been the miller).

When we kept pigs, we would never slaughter them until they were 12 stone (168 lb.) and the most usual weight was 14 stone (196 lb.). Their throats were cut and then they were hung up until the next day. Then the butcher would come, slit the pig down the middle, remove all the innards and then cut the carcass into joints.

In order to cure these, they would be put in a large wooden trough and covered with a brine mixture made with 1 pound of salt, 2 ounces of salt peter (no more than this or it makes the meat hard), 1 ounce of pepper, 1 ounce of allspice and 1 pint of strong beer. That was then turned daily for three or four weeks.

They would then be taken out, dried with a cloth, wrapped

in greaseproof paper, then a cloth and then newspaper. We could store them then for up to six months.

If there was a smoke house in the village, hams would be sent there to hang from the rafters and be smoked for two or three weeks. Oak sawdust was considered to give the best flavours.

Many farmers hung their own hams in the chimney of the backhouse – the back kitchen of the farmhouse.

Almost every part of the slaughtered cow was used, including the head.

PORK CHEESE or BRAWN

½ pig's head
fresh sage
salt and pepper
water to cover

Mrs Ashwell
Get the pig's head chopped by the butcher into manageable amounts and ensure that the cheekbone is still there. You cover the pieces with water and add sage, salt and pepper. You have to let in boil for a long time, at least three to four hours. You leave it to cool and then pick out the bones and the teeth and so on.

(Inside the pig's head are large layers of loaf fat. This is cut into pieces and separately simmered gently until it's a golden brown. Then it's strained off through muslin and pressed until cold. This makes the best lard and it's kept separately from the other fat on the pig which also makes lard - but it's less pure.)

The meat is then cut up into small pieces, the liquid in which it was boiled is strained and a pint of it is poured onto the meat, This is then boiled for half an hour. The mixture is then put into a basin and left to set overnight.

RAISED PORK PIES

Pastry	450 gr./1 lb. plain flour
	salt
	125 gr./5 ounce lard
	1 egg
	200 ml./⅓ pint water
Filling	675 gr./1½ lb. lean pork (preferably leg)
	1 teaspoonful of salt and pepper mixed
	½ teaspoonful of chopped, fresh sage
Jelly	600 ml./1 pint water
	1 pork bone (or trotter)
	½ spoonful gelatine
	salt and pepper

1. Cut the pork into small cubes and season with the salt, pepper and the sage.
2. Prepare the liquid for the jelly by putting the pork bone, the seasoning and the gelatin into the pint of cold water. Boil and then simmer for at least two hours until the liquid has been reduced to ½ pint.
3. Put the flour into a basin and add a pinch of salt. Boil the lard and water together for 5 minutes and then add to the flour, stirring it thoroughly until cold enough to be kneaded. It is important that the pastry must not get cooler than blood-heat.
4. Roll out ¾ of the pastry and line a 7" cake tin with a loose bottom. No cracks should be left in the pastry and there should be an overhang at the top so that the frill can be made.
5. Loosely fill the pastry-case with the chopped meat.
6. Roll out remaining ¼ of the pastry to make the top. Inch pleat top with the overhang, using scissors to cut off any surplus. Brush edges and top with the beaten egg. Decorate with pastry leaves.
7. Make a hole in the centre with a skewer.
8. Bake in a hot oven (Gas 6 or 400°) for ½ an hour and then reduce heat (to Gas 4 or 350°) for a further 1½ hours.

9. Remove the pork bone (or trotter) from the liquid prepared to make the jelly. Strain the liquid.
10. When pie is cooked, remove from the oven and spoon or pour as much jelly as it will hold through the central hole.
11. Leave for a least a day before eating.

PORK LOAF

100 gm./4 ounce pig's liver
1 large onion
1 stick of celery
75 gm./3 ounce of breadcrumbs
225 gm./8 ounce suet
1 teaspoon chopped sage
1 teaspoon mixed herbs
½ teaspoon marjoram
salt and pepper
1 egg yolk

1. Slice liver, put in small saucepan, pour on boiling water and simmer for 3 minutes. Drain water.
2. Peel and chop up onion. Slice celery.
3. Mince liver, pork, suet, onion and celery.
4. Add breadcrumbs, sage, mixed herbs, alt and pepper
5. Thoroughly mix in beaten egg-yolk to bind.
6. Pack into greased ½ kg./1 lb. loaf tin. Cover with greaseproof paper.
7. Put loaf tin inside a roasting tin and pour in told water to cover bottom half of loaf tin.
8. Cook in moderate oven (Gas 4 or 350°) for 1½ hours.
9. Remove from tin and serve cold.

LIVER SAVOURY

450 gm./1 lb. pig's liver
100 gm./4 ounce onions
250 gm./1 lb. potatoes

salt and pepper
powdered sage
300 ml./½ pint water

1. Wash and fry the liver and cut into thick slices. Peel and cut onions into small cubes. Peel and slice the tomatoes.
2. Cover the bottom of a greased pie dish with a layer of potato on top place slices of liver. Season well with salt, pepper and sage. Alternate with liver and potatoes until all are used, with potatoes forming the top layer.
3. Pour in the water and cover with greaseproof paper.
4. Bake in a moderate oven (Gas 3 or 325°) for 1½ hours. Then remove paper and allow the top potatoes to brown.
5. Serve with apples sauce made by simmering slowly together:
    450 gm./1 lb. apples (peeled, cored & sliced)
    40 gm./1½ ounce sugar
    25 gm./1 ounce butter
    a little water

FILLERS

As many Suffolk families were often short of food, it was common for a dish such as dumplings or Yorkshire pudding to be served with gravy as a filler before the main course.

Suffolk Dumplings (or 'Swimmers' as they were often called locally) were made from bread dough that includes yeast and milk. The dough is stood in front of the fire to rise for an hour. It is then shaped into small balls that are dropped into either boiling water or a simmering stew. After 20 minutes, they are taken out and eaten separately with gravy.

PEASE PUDDING

600 ml/1 pint split peas
40 gr/1½ oz butter
2 eggs

salt and pepper
½ teaspoon powdered sugar.

1. Soak peas in water overnight. Remove any of them that are discoloured.
2. Tie peas loosely in a pudding cloth, leaving a little room for them to swell.
3. Put them in a saucepan and cover with cold water. Bring to boiling point and then simmer for 2½ hours.
4. When peas are tender, run them through a colander with a wooden spoon.
5. Add the butter, eggs, sugar and seasoning. Mix well.
6. Tie mixture tightly into a floured cloth. Boil for another hour.
7. Turn it into a dish and serve (preferably with pieces of boiled pork).

PEASE PUDDING HOT

Poverty and The Poacher

David Peachey - born 1927
Ruby Peachey – born 1903

Although the dedication and diligence of all the farm workers I interviewed was undeniable, it is also apparent that, throughout the first half of the twentieth century, most lived in what today would be considered to be appalling poverty. Most lived in dire poverty in houses that lacked what today would be classified as rural slums – no electricity, gas, running water or even basic sanitation. How ever thorough the housekeeping was, the bare stone floors would often be covered in mud. Whether thatched or slated, the roofs would let water every time it rained. There was little enough money for food and rarely any for clothes. I have spoken to many people who went to school barefooted and their only clothes as a child were hand-downs from elder sisters or brothers.

Despite the many conversations I had with old people it was hard for me to comprehend how difficult life had been for many people, until I spoke to a man who had been a soldier at the front in the First World War.

'How on earth did you manage to put up with those conditions in the trenches – the mud, the rain, the rats and all that discomfort?' I asked.

'Weren't much different than life at home,' he said. 'And we got better food in't trenches.'

As the first half of the Twentieth Century progressed, the living conditions of rural people tended to get worse rather than better. Increasing mechanisation meant fewer jobs, as did the declining income of the aristocracy and other landowners.

Young men, when they left school, had always found it difficult to find permanent agricultural employment although there had been the possibility of casual work, such as the harvest period, when the fit and able could always find work. But as the years passed, fewer casual labourers were required.

Traditional Folk Song

THE POOR LABOURIN' MEN

Oh, some do say the farmer's best
  but I indeed say, 'No!'
If it weren't for we poor labourin' men,
  what would the farmers do?
They'd eat up all their own stuff
  until some new come in.

SWEET SORREL

There's never a trade in all England
  like we poor labourin' men.

Oh, some do say the baker's best
  but I indeed say, 'No!'
If it weren't for we poor labourin' men,
  what would the bakers do?
They'd eat up all their own stuff
  until some new come in.
There's never a trade in all England
  like we poor labourin' men.

Oh, some do say the butcher's best
  but I indeed say, 'No!'
If it weren't for we poor labourin' men,
  what would the butchers do?
They'd eat up all their own stuff
  until some new come in.
There's never a trade in all England
  like we poor labourin' men.

Let every true-born Englishman
  lift up a flowing glass
and toast each honest labourin' man -
  likewise his bonny lass.
And when these cruel days are past
  good times will come ag'in.
There's never a trade in all England
  like we poor labourin' men.

* * *

I met him for the first time one chilly, moonless night in December. I was hurrying up the long tree-vaulted lane that led to the isolated Suffolk house where we lived. I'd walked that way scores of times and had never met anyone in the lane. And I might never have seen anyone that night if I hadn't stumbled over the fallen branch of a tree.

As I lay spread-eagled in the mud, a disembodied voice came from the trees: 'Are you all right, mister?'

I wanted to run but I couldn't move. I wanted to scream but I couldn't utter a sound. In the eerie silence, I waited. I didn't hear a footstep or the crack of a twig but suddenly a strong hand grasped my shoulder.

Terrified, I bleated in an unnaturally high-pitched voice, 'I must have tripped over something.'

'You ought to be a little bit careful,' the voice said, kindly enough, 'on a night as dark as this.'

I looked up at the man who was dressed all in black and, much to my horror, was carrying a rifle. He pulled me to my feet and asked me where I was going. I told him.

'It's better if I come along with you,' he said. 'You never know what you could bump into – when it's so dark and all.'

When we arrived at my house, he willingly accepted my invitation to down some whisky and, as we entered the kitchen, I saw he was wearing a long black overcoat that hung down almost to his ankles.

While I poured the first of the many glasses we were to drink together, he took off the grubby black cap that covered most of his snow-white hair. Although had an almost unlined, burnished-red face, a slim build and mischievous bright-blue eyes, David Peachey was in his late fifties.

During that evening and the many others we spent together, he told me a great deal about his poaching activities. Although it was no longer the necessity it once had been, he continued stealthily and inconspicuously to stalk the dark country lanes on cold winter nights for the pleasure of winning yet another battle in his private war against the landowners who, with the aid of their gamekeepers, so jealously protected their hunting and shooting monopolies.

This is his story.

Well you had to hunt to live. See, when I was a lad, if it weren't for me, we wouldn't have had nothing. But I was pleased to do it, that I was. I've just got it in me, I suppose. T'was born in me – just born in me. That's all it was.

Mind you, it weren't in the rest of my family. My granddad was a straight-laced as anything, he was. He weren't no good at all as regards poaching. If he see anyone get a hare or rabbit, he'd report 'em straight away.

My dad was the same. He wouldn't do anything. He wouldn't do bugger all. He was the bloody laziest sod I've ever known. You know, he'd scorch his bum rather than move from the fire. He was a roadman. Now we're talking about forty years ago. In those days, everyone had free-range chickens, didn't they? But he cut round a nest of eggs when he was working and he'd never bring 'em home. Perhaps they'd be a hundred yards away from the farm. No-one 'ud see him, you know. No one'd see him pick 'em up. I mean, if there's half a dozen eggs in the nest, at least he could have got four, couldn't he? But no, no way he wouldn't. Bo! He'd tell me and I'd have to walk back to get 'em, you see.

During the war, a farmer at Ashfield used to keep a house-cow for butter. A lovely cow it was. The butter was about eighteen pence a pound or something like that. My dad 'ud work outside the blasted door all day but he wouldn't bring the butter home. He daren't, in case he got caught. It was the black market, you see. Everything was rationed. You wasn't allowed, you see. No, he wouldn't bring it home. So I had to walk and get it. I had to walk to bloody Ashfield 'cos I hadn't got a bike. But he'd eat the butter. Oh yes, he'd eat it afore you got in the door hardly, the old bugger. He was a rum old chap – that he was.

At home, there was no main's water. So we used to drink from the river. When I used to get home from school, my mother used to say, 'Can you go and get some water?' We used to dig a hole in the riverbed so we could put a bucket in without disturbing the sludge and whatnot. But when we got there, almost always there was a couple of ducks, bottoms-up, bibbling about in the mud so the water wasn't fit to drink. Of course, when you're thirsty, the ducks had to pay for it. So you'd kill the ducks with your catapult. It was the only way to get fresh water. So we had a lot of ducks, I can tell you!

All the meat we had at home, I brought back. We certainly couldn't afford to buy none. I'd get anything that I could lay my hands on Simple as that. Blackbirds and sparrows we used to eat. You'd pluck 'em first and take the insides out. Toast 'em in front of the fire we used to. Hang 'em on a string with a drawing pin stuck under the mantles-piece and hanging down just opposite the old basket-fire. About a dozen'd make a lovely pie. They taste delicious – really delicious they are! We used to get moorhens and peewits. Peewit eggs or plovers' eggs, we boiled or fried.

When I started work, we used to go horse hoeing with me leading the horse and a man behind steering the hoe in and out of the rows. I'd be looking down and when I came across a peewit's nest I'd stop and pick up the eggs and the man behind the horse'd call me because I was wasting time. But I'd come home with a couple or three dozen eggs in a day.

At harvest time, there were always rabbits to be caught. We young boys 'ud take sticks and, as they cut towards the centre of the field, the rabbits 'ud run out and we'd chase them with the sticks. Many a rabbit I've killed like that.

But one day a gang of us went off to a field that was near a sandpit. Now I knew all the rabbit holes were there. So I told the others that I weren't feeling too well and I'd stay in the pit. Well I blocked all the holes up inside with soil and clods of grass and, when the rabbits jumped over the pit and ran straight for their holes, they found 'em blocked up. I pulled them out by the hind legs and broke their necks. By the time the other boys came to get me, I'd got fourteen rabbits. You should have seen their faces. They were really upset I'd got more than the rest of 'em put together!

But it was all food and, in those days, we used to eat all kinds of things – sweet sorrel, we used to eat the leaves of those.

They did grow wild in the hedgerows. We always had dandelion leaves, raw like a salad. They're good for you too - plenty of iron in 'em. Then my sisters 'ud bring watercress home but I always took care of the meat.

First off, I mostly used a catapult. Mind, me dad said I couldn't have one for a long time. So I used to bury it in the garden in a tin. Made it myself, I did, from just a crotch — a bit of wood out of the hedge. I used to like elm, you know. That was stronger. But you could use ash. What we used to do with ash was (out of the way, right out of the way where no-one was likely to pass) we'd tie a potted-meat jar in the crotch and then tie the two branches together. Then we'd leave it and it'd grow to shape just perfect for a catapult.

When you've got your crutch, you bore holes through the two ends with a hot metal skewer. The rubber is the same stuff they use for the cushion on billiard tables. You could buy it from any shop. Well, you could then. You put it on with leather bootlaces. Then the stone-bag is made from shoemaker's leather. I picked the crotch up of the catapult I use now when I first started work in 1941. A while back, it split and so I had to take it to the harness makers to get it repaired. And I still use it regular like.

When I was a boy, practically everyone what lived in the country had got a catapult. You practiced at anything — telephone-cups what used to be on the poles. Practically anything. I was soon killing things. You name it and I brought it home. I got really good at it.

That's why me dad changed his mind about me having a catapult. One night, just after I'd left school when I was about fourteen, I come home from the Ashfield Swan, full of beer or something like that, and there was a blue-tit sittin' on the window-sill of our house. Course out come me catapult. How the hell I done it I shall never know. I just don't know how I done it. But I got it, just like that, even though I'd shot straight at the bloody window. Well my dad had been watching and he says, 'Well, boy, if you can use a catapult like that you deserve to 'ave one!' After that, I always had a catapult with me and I made use of it a lot.

With a pheasant, you've just got to hit the head and that's it. I've had 'em flying. But, of course, that's pure luck – no question about it, that's pure luck. I've shot, well, nine or ten flying. They get up and away they go and then you just take potluck and if they fall that's your good fortune. But most time you've got to wait for 'em to walk up to you. You've got to sit under cover and wait for them to come to you, which they'll do quite often.

I've had foxes look me straight in the face just a couple of feet away. You've got to be still. I've even had kingfishers sit on my fishing-line. It's surprising what I've done.

Mind, my best success with a catapult was at the Ashfield *Swan*. Gordon Woods bet me I couldn't hit three matchsticks with three shots from eight yards. He was a catapult man, although he used ball bearings. I couldn't get on with 'em. I like an egg-shaped stone. Anyhow, he stuck three matches in a bar of Sunlight soap. Well, I took 'em out one at a time – and I'd had several pints! I was about eighteen then, I suppose.

In fact, even later when I was shooting and there was a rabbit on the seat, I'd lay my gun down and pull my catapult out. I was sure of it but I weren't at first with a gun.

The first time I started shooting, I had a popgun. I made it out of a piece of elder. You see, everything we had, we had to make. When I went to school, we hadn't any money at all. There weren't any money about. But a popgun's easy to make. You get a piece of elder and drive the pith out. Then you make a stick to go right through it. You stick an acorn in one end, the widest end, and drive it up to the other end as far as it will go. Then you put another acorn in and drive that up with air in between the two acorns. Then you push it against you. The acorn'll go fifty yards easily, just like that! And smoke! It'd smoke just like a twelve-bore. Mind you, you wouldn't kill anything with it, although I once nearly killed my mother with it. I shot at her and hit her right on the ankle. The acorn had a little point on it and her ankle really went black and blue. She cussed at me, that she did!

I first got a shotgun just after I left school at fourteen. My dad didn't approve if it. No way! He nearly cut his throat the first time I used it. That's honest. I bought it off a chap in Debenham. He wanted six pounds for it but I said, 'No, that's too much!'

And then I saw him in the *Cherry Tree* one night and he say, 'Are you still interested in the old gun?'

And I say, 'Not at six pounds.'

He say, 'Have you got any money on you? I'm stony broke. Haven't got a bean.'

So I said, 'Sell me the old gun then. I'll give you four for the old gun.'

'That's done,' he say.

So I got the old gun for four pounds.

Then I took it home and I had one bloody hell of a row when I took it in. 'What you going to do with that?' my dad said.

And I said, 'Use it! On anything that moves!'

The chap who lived next door used to have free-range chickens and there was netting to stop them coming through to our place. Of course, we used to lift the netting and, with a bit or two of bread, they'd come through right enough. Well I looked though our open kitchen window and there was one of his chickens in our garden. So I lifted up the gun and shot it – bang!

My dad was a-shavin' at the time and he did jump. 'Bloody hell!' he said and he called me left, right and centre. But there you are, I kept the gun and he ate the chicken I can tell you.

Since then I've had some good catches. The most pheasant I ever shot at one time was twenty-four. Mind you, I knew where the man bred them! That was about two in the morning. There wasn't any moon. (You never go out on a moonlit night. They can see you. It's like going out in broad daylight.) I got all those with an air gun. You've got to have a torch. You see the bird sit, take aim, on go the torch. Bang! Then you either hit or you miss. If you've hit, that's yours. If you miss, that's gone.

But there isn't as much game around now. When I was a lad, every clump of grass had got a rabbit in, on the seat. Rabbits always make a proper seat. They don't just sit anywhere, you know. They make their seat, the rabbit do. They hammer it down till they're comfortable, because I've watched them do it. 'Cos I've sat for hours and hours in the hedgerows. Hundreds of hours I've sat watching 'em.

And it's amazing what you can see. I've even seen hares run my dog off the field. Honestly I have. Yes, and it's really been frightened. Perhaps there were seven or eight hares - you know at March time when they're breeding. My dog looked like a hare – same colour, practically the same. It was a little terrier. Anyway, it ran right back to me, terrified. If it'd been only one hare on its own, my dog'd have had it. But there were so many of 'em. It was eight to one. But that's how it go, I suppose.

You know, if you see a hare on the seat, you could practically walk up to 'em and pick 'em up. On two occasions, I've walked the dog and that's stood right on the hare before it got up. Just like that! Oh, they'll sit 'cos they can't see in front of them. It's true! Hares can't see in front of 'em when they're sitting. They can see sideways and behind. If you walk straight up to it on the seat and if you're quiet, you can walk within a yard easy. Well, plenty of hares I've just walked up to and struck 'em. And that's it. Just with a stick. But you've got to be right for the wind. Well, everything's got to be right, hasn't it?

The best dog I ever had was Gypsy, a Norfolk Lurcher. She could get no end of hares. Brilliant at it, Gypsy was. You see, when a hare runs, it keeps just far enough ahead of the dog, then it turns sharply and most dogs will keep straight on or turn in a curve so they lose the hare. But Gypsy could turn as sharply as a hare. One night alone, she caught fourteen. I could barely carry them – well, of course, I couldn't carry them all at once! But I sold them to the butcher for five bob a piece.

I've also used nets and snares to catch rabbits. Going up

the lane to school, I'd always put some snares on the hedge and, when I cam back, as like as not there'd be a rabbit in one of them. You just put the snares where the rabbit had been coming through. You'd know where that was 'cos you could see bits of fur on the bushes. That's how it is. You've got to be a keen observer, I suppose. You've got to spend a long time alone. You listen, observe and know every stick and stone where you hunt.

The snares you just bought in a hardware or hunting shop. They're made of copper wire with an eyelet at the end. You bend 'em pear-shape, not round. They've got to be pear-shape. There's an art in that. There's an art in snaring, there's no doubt about it.

Then you put the snares in a rabbit run. A rabbit has a special run you can see. They hop, hop, and where they land there's a dent in the ground. They're very distinct they are. And you put the snare in the middle between the dents 'cos runs are very distinct. I've seen a rabbit on the seat and, knowing the area, I think, 'Well, the holes are over there and the rabbit's there. So I'll put a snare here.' I'll go round to make the rabbit run that way and, no trouble at all, the snare catches it just like that. A hundred per cent sure, you see.

A couple of years back, I went to my old mate's for dinner one Christmas Day and he said, 'We've got to go and put some snares down.' Anyhow, we put fifty-four snares for rabbits. I know you'll never believe it. That seems really impossible to do. But how many d'you think we picked up on Boxing Day? Fifty-two and, we could see from the tufts of fur, one got away!

Then many, many a night I've been out with a drag net. That's about fifty foot long and about thirty foot wide. It's just ordinary netting. You've got to have a partner with you. Then you just keep walking and walking till you hear something get up - a covey of partridges or something like that – and you drop the net immediately. Then all you do is just walk to wherever in the net they might be. That's it and they're all yours. You could have caught two or twenty. It all depends how big the covey is.

Years ago, there used to be plenty of partridges but not

any more due to sprays and whatnot. They do away with birds, don't they? Must do. There's no doubt about it, if it weren't for the breeders, I don't think there's be any pheasants at all. They're much less rabbits than there were. I mean, when I was courting, I always had nets with me and a catapult. Every time! All my mind was on rabbits! Every pipe I came across I used to have a look up. We even used to tie fireworks on a stick, set light to it and push it in as far as it would go and then bang! Out would come the rabbit right into the net. No trouble at all!

Over the years, I've shot thousands of rabbits and hares and not all at night I can tell you. My best was when the local doctor here used to rent a shoot at the Hall. I used to watch his motor so that I knew when he was there. Then I'd go into the neighbouring field. His dog, he had no control of it at all. And he couldn't even hit the ground with a twelve-bore. So he used to put up the hares and they used to come right through the hedge and I used to stand there and bang! Every time a winner! Couldn't lose!

Then he said to me, 'They're my hares.'

I said, 'Well come after them and you'll get the same as the bloody hares!'

One day, I was just off shooting and I was walking up the street with a twelve-bore. The butcher came out of his shop with a tray of eggs and he said, holding and egg up, 'Pound you can't hit it!'

I said, 'Hang on! I haven't got no cartridges in yet.' So I stuck in a couple of cartridges in and said, 'Right! Throw it reasonable – out of the sun and everything else. Be fair!'

'Right oh!' he said and threw one up and bang! I got that. He threw another and bang! I got that one too.

That night, the police came after me for shooting on the highway. But I didn't mind – I'd got the butcher's pound!

But I've never had too much trouble with the police. One day, the policeman's wife did come to the door and asked me if I'd got a gun. I said, 'Yes. You should know that. Your husband knows I've got one in any case. Why do you want to know?'

'Well,' she said, 'we've got some rabbits in our garden. They're eating all my flowers off. D'you think you could get 'em for me?'

'I'll have a go,' I said.

So I went, two or three mornings very early, five o'clock time. But I never saw no rabbit. So the next time, I took a dead rabbit with me and ruffled it up so that it was a bit limp. I threw it over the fence. Then I had two shots right past the policeman's bedroom window.

Gor blimey, he looked out of there and said, 'Whatever are you doing?'

'Shooting rabbits,' I said. 'Your wife has said they're eating everything that's in the garden.'

'Well,' he said. 'Did you get it?'

'Yes,' I said. 'I thinks so. It should be on that meadow somewhere.' So I walked round and pretended to hunt high and low for it. Then I picked up the dead rabbit and said, 'Here it is!'

He was right pleased. And, do you know, his misses never had any more trouble with rabbits!

Of course, the gamekeepers have always been more trouble. They're just ordinary people and yet they're a damned sight keener than the people what own the land. They're always on the watch but you've just got to find out their whereabouts. It's as simple as that.

Once, Russel Baker, who was a gamekeeper for Mr Short, asked me if I'd sweep his chimney.

When I called on him, a pheasant got up on a tree. 'Go t'hell!' I said. 'Just look at that! Have you got a gun?'

And he said, 'Of course I have.'

I said, 'Well go and get it. We'll have that pheasant.'

'No!' he said. 'It's nothing to do with you. It's nothing to do with me. 'Tisn't mine and 'tain't yourn!'

I said, 'It will be if you get the gun!'

But he said, 'If you shoot that, d'you know what I'd do?'

I said, 'No.'

'Well,' he said, 'first I'd ring Mr Short and then the police.'

'Well,' I said, 'get the bloody gun quick and let me get it.'

'No,' he said.

'Well, it'd pay you really,' I said. 'If you'd let me get the pheasant and then you ring the police and Mr Short, they'd be sure to come up here, wouldn't they?'

He said, 'Of course they would!'

I said, 'Well then you could get 'em to sweep your bloody chimney because I'm not! Anyhow, you don't want to worry. You go to whist-drives every Tuesday night, don't you?'

He said, 'Yes.'

'Well, that's it. I'll come back on Tuesday night. You've got plenty of pheasants round here. I'll just get one for myself.'

Well, he never went to another whist drive! If I never live to see my wife again, that's the truth!

Though the gamekeepers could be a bit of a nuisance, I've never had much trouble with the landowners. A few years back, I was walking up towards the Hall when I saw a rabbit run into a pipe under the road. I thought, 'I'm going to get that.' So I got out my net from my bag and put it over one end of the pipe.

Just then Mr Grace, who owned the Hall, came along. 'What you doing then?' he said.

'Getting this rabbit,' I said.

'There's no rabbit in there,' he said. 'We've just had a

shoot over here.'

'Yes, there is,' I said. Then I looked up the pipe but it was empty. But I knew the rabbit was still about. Leading from the catch-pit was a small length of pipe running into the field. The rabbit must have jumped into there and stayed. So I poked a stick up and the rabbit ran out.

Mr Grace shot it and then brought it over to me. 'There's you rabbit,' he said.

'No, thanks,' I said. 'I'm not having it.'

'Why not?' he said.

'Well let's get this straight,' I said. 'I'll have what I get and you have what you get!'

'Oh, no!' he said, 'cos he knew me. 'I'm not having any of that! There's no way I'm having you deciding what's your and what's mine in this world! So pick up the rabbit! It's yours!'

So I touched my cap and walked off – with the rabbit.

* * *

For centuries, the sole right of landowners to kill the wild game on their land and catch the fish in their waters had been protected not only by their gamekeepers but also by laws that have classified poaching as being one of the most serious criminal offences. Yet driven often by poverty rather than greed, many country people regularly out-witted the gamekeepers and flouted the law so they could provide otherwise unobtainable meat and fish for their families.

So, although farm-workers had traditionally accepted their position in an almost feudal agricultural system, the poacher refused to accept that wild animals, birds and fish were the rightful property of the person on whose land they happened to be found.

Today, there no longer exists the severe poverty endured in most rural areas. Today, there are very few farm-workers and the rural villages where once they lived now provide dormitory residences for affluent town workers. Today, game is far harder to find than once it was – rabbits were decimated by myxomatosis and few landowners are prepared to go to the trouble and expense of rearing pheasants. Today, the traditional poacher has all but disappeared.

THE POACHER AND HIS DOG

I've got me a dog and a good dog too
and I hold her in me keeping.
Me and me dog goes out at night
whilst them keepers lie a-sleeping.
Me and me dog went out last night
for to l'arn some education.
Up jumps a hare and away she runs
right into the old plantation.

She hadn't gone not so very far
when me dog she stopped her running.
'Oh, help me, help me!' the hare did cry.
'For them keepers lie a-sleeping.'
But I takes me out me old sharp knife
and there and then I did slay her.
That's how she ended her roaming life.
How glad I am that I caught her.

I picks her up and I smooths her down.
Secure she was in my keeping.
I says to me dog, 'Let's be a-going
whilst them keepers lie a-sleeping.'
Away me and me old dog did run
back home into sweet Debenham town.
We took the hare to the butcher's house
and sold her for a silver crown.

Then we called into the public house
where we bought some ale quite mellow.
We spent that crown and another one too
'cos I'm a stout-hearted fellow.

> I've got this dog and a good dog too
> and I hold her in me keeping.
> Me and me dog goes out at night
> whilst them keepers lie a-sleeping.

It was, of course, the wives of both unemployed and working farm labourers who endured the brunt of the rural deprivation caused by poverty, isolation and inadequate living conditions. Often born into large families, most village girls, during their brief period of schooling, shared the household chores and childcare with their mothers and sisters. After leaving school, they had but a brief period of employment before they married and then brought up their own families. It was all but impossible for them ever to find any paid employment.

Ruby Peachey, David's mother, was in her mid-eighties when we met in 1980 and had been a widow for ten years. She had lived in the same small cottage in the small hamlet of Framsden for over fifty years. It had no bathroom or inside toilet and was some five miles from the nearest village centre. Despite this, she had a fund of often happy memories and a most infectious sense of humour.

I was born in Shingle Street in Debenham. There were seven of us children at home. And in this house in Debenham, we used to have the floods.

Well you can picture nine of us, can't you? We had to live upstairs for a week. Soon as it began to rain a little, the old river flood 'ud come up right through the street, right straight through yer house every time there was a fairly heavy shower. It didn't want to take much for the damn stuff to come all over the road and round the corner. We used to hear it come.

My father he'd sit ag'in the back door. I can see him now, poor old chap. He'd sit there and say, 'Yes, that's a-comin' in tonight!'

You'd watch it comin' up, inch by inch up the wall. We had to pick up all the things and take as much water as we could upstairs. The chairs had to be on top of the table and then the sofa – all on top of each other.

Then we had to take the ferrets upstairs, the chickens upstairs and the dog upstairs. We had three rooms upstairs and we all had to live up there. The milkman used to come round with a horse and tumbril and pass the milk through the bedroom window.

It please us kids 'cause we never had to go to school. That might last a week at a time. And the muck it used to leave behind! Cor blimey, the house stunk for weeks. Gracious, yes! It had to be scrubbed right through. All the carpets, everything, had to come right up. And it wasn't just us. All the houses in our row got it. But nobody did nothin' about the floods. You just had to take it as it come.

I was fourteen when I left school and went to work in Abbott's shop. That was a lot better than being at school! I learnt all the tricks of the trade – weighin' up things and servin' people behind the counter. We used to have to wrap everythin' up in a sheet of brown paper when people came to buy 'em. Lot of people couldn't make a parcel of it but I could. If you'd got twenty things, I could pack 'em up so you could carry 'em on the back of yer bike. You'd got to then. Nine out of ten people, that's how they'd come down – on their bikes.

Saturday night, there'd be lines of men standin' outside the window, puttin' their fingers up to me.

I'd say, 'Come on in and buy somethin'!'

They'd come in and say, 'Well, darlin', we want two pen'orth of peppermint balls!'

I'd say, 'Do you? D'you want black uns, white uns or red uns?'

There stood me boy friend – the man I married – standin' outside lookin' just like daggers. He didn't like me a-carryin' on. I met him when I was about sixteen. He used to come down into the village and he'd be peepin' through the shop window and that's how we met.

I was nineteen when I got married. We hadn't two ha'pennies to rub together either. I said, 'Oh, we're going to get hitched, are we? Who's goin' to buy the ring?'

He said, 'Well if you've got the money, you'll have to!'

I said, 'That's cheerful, i'n't it?'

Course, work was very difficult then, that time of day, for men as well as boys leavin' school. He had no job and there was no dole or nothin'. You had to wait till a job came along at the farm or somethin' like that. After we got married, he was out of work for several years.

At first, when we got married, we stayed with his parents but it got so they had to move out. The farm changed hands and he'd got to go. The family moved down to Thorndon and I went with 'em. That's where me first baby was born. But then we had to get 'our own place and we moved to just up the road near here. Till he got a job, the only money we had was what he got playin' the accordion and singin' in pubs. He got to get money from somewhere and they was quite free at that time of day – more free than they are today. He'd take as much in one night as he would workin' in a week. Somebody'd always take the hat round. But he only went out chiefly on Saturday evenings. It wasn't every night.

Oh, I couldn't stick that. I told him, 'If you go out every Saturday, I shall have somebody else in! I shan't sit alone!'

Mind, they weren't all that late home, you know. And there weren't the goin's-on there are today. You'd sleep with yer backdoor open. You wouldn't think about anybody comin' in.

Mind you, most of the time I had a neighbour. That makes a lot of difference. The old man next door'd come home for work and hear me whistlin'. He'd holler, 'Ere, Ruby,' (I was as big as a brewing tub but still that didn't seem to matter!) 'Yew sound happy,' he'd say. 'What? Has the old man been home?'

I'd say, 'You get indoors and see to yer old woman!'

Mind, wa'n'y long before I had to call his old woman in and tell her what her old man was after! Aye, such is life! I like to have somebody to swear at when I get riled!

We didn't have much food ever. I used to say we have just a piece of 'bread an' pullit'. (He'd get on one end of the bread and I'd get on the other and we'd just pull it! That made it go further!)

Course, we had more than that! We had goats. So we had plenty of lovely milk. We used to make butter by shakin' the milk up in a jam-jar. It'd only take a quarter if an hour. If I could buy a pound of rice, that was what we chiefly lived on – rice puddin's.

When we had four pence to spare, we'd manage to get a loaf. And we'd eat a lot of swedes – boiled. My hubby used to buy the swedes at about sixpence a hundredweight for the goats. Some of his old mates what used to go drinkin' with him would 'ave allotments and he'd get the swedes from them. But we ate them as well as the goats and jolly good grub too, I can tell you! never taste 'em like that now. I think meself that be because of all the stuff they put now on the land.

Then I bought some scrap drippin', when I'd got a tanner to spare. It was lovely – just like lard. You could spread it like butter. You see you've got the flavour of the meat in it. It were beautiful. Bit of salt and pepper on it and you were well away.

Then we kept rabbits and killed one of them when we was hungry. We went in for rabbits – kept them in cages outside. Chiefly, I'd make a rabbit pie and, if I could afford it, I'd buy a piece of belly pork and put that in with it. That made it a lot better.

There used to be horse-and-carts, then vans, come round from the butchers. There were plenty of 'em runnin' around then.

Course, we were often hungry but we were always healthy. Couldn't afford the luxuries they do today. And we was a lot better of for it, in regards health. Well, I think so anyway.

Most of the time I was in the house with the young

children. I didn't get out of the village much. Mind, my parents lived in Debenham and say once a week I used to walk there with the pram. I knew where to go 'cause me mum was better off than me. She'd sort of set me up with a bag of cakes or somethin' to come home with. Mother could bake — that was one thing about her. She used to bake her own bread about twice a week 'cause there were nine of us at home. She used to make it and they'd come round and collect it and take it up to the baker's, cook it and bring it back.

I didn't have any friends. I didn't see many other women. Chance time you might see the odd one — wasn't very often. I was nearly all day cleanin' up behind the children. When they'd gone to school and I went for a walk, I went by myself — like I do now. I used to walk a couple of miles each way along the lane pickin' up wood and sticks to light the fire with.

I put wheels on an old loafsugar box — I still got it. Well you'd got to do somethin' to keep warm, hadn't you? That was all extras so you don't have to buy no coal. Yes, lookin' after everything was a full-time job. You never thought about a part-time job or anything like that.

And clothes we used to go without. We couldn't buy any. So chiefly we had 'em give us by relatives - all second-hand. 'Hand-me-downs' they call 'em. I had some lovely clothes given me. Thank God, I was taught to sew at school. I used to make all the little trousers and shirts out of big garments given me - and the same with the dresses for the girls.

Course, I knew the farmers and that like were better off than me. But I didn't mind. What was the good? It was no good me a-sayin' I'd leave me husband 'cause he couldn't get no money or he couldn't get nor work. My mother didn't want me home 'cause she always had six other children. I couldn't go there. So we just had to grin and bear it — make the best of it. Well you do, don't you? Today, they just split off and part and that's that. Wasn't the same in my time. You knew you were stuck with what you'd got and that's all there was to it.

Families like the Peachey's never had much money. This not only meant that it was never possible to buy clothes for themselves or the children and it was often difficult to put adequate amounts of food on the table, it also meant they could never think of paying for a doctor to visit, for a stay in hospital or for any medicines. Families dreaded any of its members dying because they would not have sufficient means to pay for the funeral. For the members of most rural families, paupers' graves were inevitably their final resting places.

Without access to professional medical aid, rural families had to rely on folk medicines and traditional superstitions. These are some of the remedies that Ruby Peachey used and recommended.

ARTHRITIS
1. Steam asparagus and drink the water.
2. Eat celery seeds.
3. Drink potato juice to relieve pain.
4. To reduce the pain, drink a cup of hot water to which is added a tablespoonful of vinegar and a teaspoonful of honey.

BOILS
1. Apply hot bread to bring boil to a head.
2. Place a slice of onion on the boil to draw out infection.

BRONCHITIS
1. Drink fresh cabbage juice daily.
2. Simmer vinegar in a little water, cover your head with a towel and inhale.

CRAMP
1. Sleep with a cork under the pillow.
2. Carry a small piece of sheep's bone in your pocket.
3. Put your shoes upside down before going to bed.

CUTS
1. Bathe it with your own urine to prevent infection.
2. Sprinkle table salt on it.

3. Bind on a slice of horseradish to encourage healing.
4. Apply warm bread to an infected cut to limit itching.

EARACHE
1. Hold a hot onion to the ear.
2. Dissolve table salt in lukewarm water and drop into ear to dissolve wax.
3. Put a few drips of warm urine into the ear.
4. Sit with your head close to the fire or a hot oil lamp.

EYE COMPLAINTS
1. Rub with your own spittle early in the morning before eating.
2. Rub a stye with a gold wedding ring that you have first licked.
3. Rub eyelid with the tip of a black cat's tail.
4. Sniff pepper to make you sneeze.
5. Eat a raw carrot daily.
6. For eye infections, use drops of honey water.
7. Apply cold bread to reduce eye irritation and swelling.

HEADACHES
1. Bathe forehead with warm water in which mint, sage or vinegar has been boiled.
2. Wear a viper's head and skin around your head.
3. To stop, lie down and put a coin on your heart.
4. Place on your back a large key or scissors, points up.
5. Sniff a puff-ball.

MOUTH SORES & ULCERS
1. Dab on a little white cabbage juice.
2. Eat fresh apples.
3. Drop on a few drops of fresh lemon juice.

RHEUMATISM
1. Boil cucumbers whole in a large pot with a little salt. After they have simmered for an hour, remove and extract the juice. A week later, the liquid can be applied on a wet flannel to the affected part.
2. Drink poppy tea (made from the seeds of white poppies).
4. Carry around a piece of an animal's anklebone.

An outside Suffolk 'privy' – the toilet in an outside shed.
The torn pieces of newspaper are ready for use!

Alf Peachey

Village Pubs

In the first half of the twentieth century, the male-only village pubs were the centres of the cultural and social life of the workingmen in every rural village. Especially on Saturday evenings, it was where the men of the village not only drank strong and - before greedy breweries succeeded in exerting their monopoly - home-brewed beers but also talked, played a wide variety of games, sang and danced, fought bare-fisted at the slightest provocation and, for a few hours, escaped from their everyday life of poverty and almost unending physical toil.

In the days when, in the villages, there were no cinemas or television, it was the village pubs that provided the men's entertainment. It was there that local musicians played and sang.

Ruby's husband, Alf Peachey, was one of the most famed local musicians. He died in 1970. For 43 years, he had been a council roadman, employed to repair the many holes in the road *and keep the drainage functioning. He was always poorly paid and, despite Ruby's valiant efforts and their son David's poaching, it had always been difficult to provide adequate food for the large family.*

However, throughout his married life, he had supplemented his meager income by earning money, as he was doing when he first me Ruby, by playing his melodeon (which unlike an accordion had only buttons and not a keyboard) and singing in many pubs around Framsden. All the old men I spoken to agreed that he was the best local musician they had ever heard. He was, it is said, 'a local legend in his life-time'.

David Peachy spoke to me about his father and his accordion.

Well, on that melodeon, he was self-taught but, no doubt about it, he was brilliant.

He got started when he was very young. When he was about five, his mother cut him one out of paper, all crimpled up. He was accordion crazy. Then they bought him one for Christmas or somethin' like that. It only had three buttons or so but it made a noise. Well, he started from there. He was one of the very best. He was all self-taught. He didn't know a note of music at all – nothin'. But he could really make the thing talk, there's no doubt about it.

D'you know, during the First World War, he were a young soldier – must have been one of the youngest. They do say that in the trenches, other soldiers carried his rifle and all his kit so he could play his accordion. He was able to make it sound like the bagpipes which must have been a bit confusin' to those Jerries! (I'll tell you somethin'. D'you know why they were called 'Jerries'? It was 'cause they wore those 'elmets that looked like a chamber-pot and everybody called those 'jerries'!)

Well, none of us boys was allowed to even touch Dad's accordion or there'd be right trouble. He used to keep it in an old army valise and he'd wrap it all around in long scarfs. When you looked at it, you'd think it was right new, even though he'd had it for more than forty years.

He sang non-stop. He would sing and play. Not many people do. But he would sing all the time. He'd accompany hisself. Well, he used to get free beer and then with the hat they'd collect round from the customers. So he'd bring home ten or fifteen shillings – somethin' like that. That was a lot of money those days. Then, in the pubs, he drank gallons and gallons – no doubt about it.

He used to specialise in hornpipes, which was for the step-dancing. Most of them were Irish but he learned them all off records. All his songs he learned from records. When he came home at night, he'd put the records on. He had an old wind-up gramophone with a horn and he used to turn the horn towards the stairs door. Course, us kids used to go to bed about eight. So we heard the songs in bed and we learned them as well as he did. And some of them were beautiful songs – beautiful songs. They brought tears to your eyes, they did.

He could play anythin' – step-dance tunes, hornpipes, reels, waltzes, marches. You name it: he'd play it. He'd even play and sing tunes like 'The Man on the Flying Trapeze' and 'Home on the Range'. Harry Lauder was one of his real favourites.

You name it, there ain't a pub he ain't been in within a twenty-five five radius. The Ashfield *Swan* and the Framsden *Greyhound* were his favourites but he played everywhere – Worlingworth, Debenham, Framlingham.

He would never play for dances – just mainly at weddings and darts matches. He liked a good crowd, you see. Many a time, he'd cycle to a pub where there was a darts match and get his accordion out and, after that, not a dart would be thrown all night! He could 'ave worked all the time but he'd only play when he wanted and that only on a Friday or Saturday. He did play at all his mates' weddings and at mine.

I used to go around with him a lot. He was always very

popular. He was a sturdy man with happy face and a big dimple in his chin. A bit of a joker and always fond of his beer, the blokes in the pubs loved him. When he wasn't singing, he smoked a long down-curving pipe.

Dad might have not been able to read music but he had a great ear. When he'd heard a song he liked, he could play it straight off. He also knew if there was the slightest thing wrong with his accordion. He had a reed go and took it to be repaired. They put in a piano accordion reed – and the piano accordion is a different instrument from dad's that had no keyboard. After that, he hardly ever played it – he thought people would know.

One night in 1970, we were down the *Swan* and Dad played for a while but I thought some'ut was up because it was the first time I'd ever seen him stumped to finish his beer. The next day, he died.

This is one of Alf Peachey's favourite songs.
THE RAT-CATCHER'S DAUGHTER

(Although there were probably much earlier versions, the song was certainly sung in American music halls at the end of the nineteenth century.)

>Now not long ago in Westminster,
>there lived a rat catcher's daughter.
>But perhaps it weren't in Westminster
>'cause she lived t'other side of the water.
>Her father killed rats, while she sold sprats
>all around and about that quarter.
>And the young gentlemen all raised their hats
>to the pretty, little rat-catcher's daughter.
>   Doodledum! Doodledee! Didum doodleldee!
>
>She bore no hat upon her head –
>no hat, no perky bonnet.

SWEET SORREL

While down her back her hair did fall
like a bunch of carrots upon it.
When she cried 'Sprats' in Westminster,
she had a beautiful voice, sir.
You could hear her all through Parliament Street
as far as Charing Cross, sir.
    Doodledum! Doodledee! Didum doodleldee!

Now rich and poor, both far and near,
in matrimony sought her.
But she turned up her nose at all the lot,
did the pretty little rat-catcher's daughter,
for she knew a man sold lily-white sand,
in Cupid's naked quarter.
And head over heels in love with him,
was the pretty, little rat-catcher's daughter.
    Doodledum! Doodledee! Didum doodleldee!

Now Lily-white-sand so ran in her head
as she went along the Strand-oh,
she forgot that she'd got sprats on her head
and cried, 'D'you want any lily-white sand, oh?'
The folks amazed all thought her crazed
as she went along the Strand-oh,
to see a girl with sprats on her head
cry, 'D'you want any lily-white sand, oh?'
    Doodledum! Doodledee! Didum doodleldee!

Now Lily-white-sand was just as bad.
He couldn't think what he was after.
Instead of crying about lily-white sand,
said, 'Do you want any rat-catcher's daughter?'
His donkey cocked his ears and brayed –
that's the donkey's way of laughter –
to hear his friend and master cry,
'Do you want any rat-catcher's daughter?'

Now they both agree to married be
upon next Easter Sunday
but the rat-catcher's daughter she had dreamt
that she wouldn't be alive on Monday.
She went once more to buy some sprats
and tumbled into the water
and down to the bottom of the dirty Thames
went the pretty little rat-catcher's daughter.
   Doodledum! Doodledee! Didum doodleldee!

Now when Lily-white-sands had heard the news,
his eyes ran down with water
and he said, 'My love, I'll constant prove.
I'll be blowed if I live long after.'
So he cut his throat with a square of glass
and he stabbed his donkey also.
And that was the end of Lily-white-sand
and the donkey and the rat-catcher's daughter.
   Doodledum! Doodledee! Didum doodleldee!

It was not just the melodeon soloist who played in the village pubs. Others played concertinas, mouthorgans, fiddles and banjos. And it wasn't just the soloist who sang. Everybody was expected to join in and there were many of the old men who had their favourite songs they wanted to sing.

*   Another part of the communal entertainment in Suffolk village pubs was step-dancing. It was a form of tap dancing usually performed by an individual male, often to a hornpipe tune. It was an improvised dance without any fixed pattern of steps. Some held their arms rigid to their sides while others waved them about quite a lot. The sound and rhythm of the steps was the most important element. Indeed, it is said that when competitions were held, the judges were often below in the beer cellar so they saw nothing – they only heard the sounds of the steps.*

A wooden base was necessary to produce the best sound. Some dancers had Blakey's (a small metal plate) in the heels of their shoes. In some pubs, an old wooden door was produced for the dancer.

David Peachey

When you're step-dancing, all you do is just tap your feet. It's like playing the drums. Some keep still above the knees; others are all on the go. It's different. It all depends. There's definitely a lot of difference in people's step-dancing. If you use your whole body, your legs don't hurt so much. But it's always on the same spot. We used to put a tray down or a bit of wood if the floor weren't good enough. Or maybe you've got the wrong shoes on and you've got to have something to make the taps.

Nobody taught me how to step-dance. I just taught meself 'cause I was never a man to keep still. There used to be competitions in the pubs. I was never fortunate enough to win one but I used to go in for them. Down *The Cherry Tree* in Debenham they had them.

There were always accordions goin' in practically every pub. Mind, I didn't play one. I used to play the bones. I made my own out of oak. Really they should be bollock rib-bones but I couldn't get any wide enough to hold. So mine are oak.

* * *

Although visiting musicians might be welcomed, almost every village pub was a closed community and strangers were treated with suspicion. Even people from neighbouring villages would be treated with mistrust and a word out of place or a quibble about different rates of pay would quickly lead to an invitation to 'step outside'. It was never a no-holds-barred, vicious scrap with kicking and wrestling holds. Good, clean fisticuffs was the norm and, if the pair were well matched, the bare-knuckled contest might go on for an hour or more, much to the enthusiastic delight of the encircling crowd. At the end, the hat would be passed round and often the victor would share his spoils with the loser.

The local policeman, who more often than not was himself a local, would rarely intervene. He knew well who were the bad 'uns in the neighbourhood and he kept his eye on them.

David Steele of Bedfield gave me this account of a policeman's intervention.

At Monk Soham *Elm*, there was an old boy in there a-arguin' the point about this and one thing an' another. The policeman come in there and said, 'Come on, Freeman. Out you come. I've 'ad enough o' you!'

He said, 'You can't put me out!'

Well that policeman got 'old of 'im by the scruff of his neck, shoved 'im out and stuck his boot up his behind. Well Freeman he went down them three steps out of Monk Soham *Elm* and he never touched on of 'em! He land in't middle o' the road!

About a week afterwards, we see Freeman down Earl Soham and, 'Come in there, Freeman, and sit down. You make the place look untidy!'

He said, 'I dussun't.'

He was afraid, you see. Afraid of the policeman!

* * *

As was normally the case in the villages, the policeman earned respect not because he was the guardian of the law but because he was able to deal physically with those who were causing trouble. Of course, he had to keep on his toes because some men, especially the young, would try to get the better of the village copper.

Cooker Carver

We all stood on Earl Soham corner 'bout eight o'clock one Sat'day night. There was no end of people and boys about. Policeman

Howard was policeman in the village.

Now old Sonny Warne had a little old gun. Now he and Arthur Reed and I were three little buggers together. We stood ag'in the corner and Sonny Warne said to me, 'Go and stand up ag'in that chimney and let that gun off!'

Course, all these old men were standin' about talkin', but I said, 'All right!'

Well, of course, us three went up the lane. We knew Howard was there – we could see his buttons a-shinin'. So they said, 'We'll look out then. We know where we'll run to if he comes after us.'

Well, of course, I let the gun off. You talk about jumpin' and hoppin' about! Everybody was a-shoutin' and a-hollerin'.

And off we went with old Howard runnin' behind us like hell. We went across the little green and the bottom of the park and down the drift towards the river. Howard was thumpin' behind us and we'd got over the river and out the other side.

When we got to the osier beds *(a place where willows are grown for basket making)*, I said to Arthur Reed, 'You go back over that far bloody side and I'll hide here and, when he's passed over, I'll pull the bloody bridge up.'

So I sat in the reeds and wait till he come clompin' over this here bridge after us. When he got over that bridge, I walked back over it and pulled the bugger up.

Course, Howards was stuck in the osier beds and us three went into the back of the *Falcon*. We kept listenin' and listenin'. After a little while, Howard come into the bar and he said, 'Have you seen any bloody boys come in here?'

They said, 'What boys?'

He said, 'I don't know yet.' Then he comes through the back, through the kitchen and passed us old boys. 'You're all right there then,' he says.

'Yes,' I said. 'We're all right. Aren't you then?'

He said, 'Yes, I'm all right.' But he was soakin' from head to foot and his old uniform was drippin' wet.

He never did find out who it was. Nobody did tell him who'd pulled the bloody bridge up!

The absurdity of the British licensing-laws (introduced somewhat vindictively by the Government during the First World War to prevent excessive drinking among munitions workers) has, at times, caused conflict between villagers and the police, especially in more recent times, after the local bobby had been replace by policemen from out of the area driving around in their flash cars.

However, even in the mid-1970s, when I was living in Bedfield, the police normally ignored the more remote rural public houses, frequented only by locals, even though, especially on Saturday evenings, drinks were often sold much later than the permitted hour. Occasionally, however, the police have been known to arrive.

Once, a good three hours after the legal closing time, about twenty off us were still merrily drinking in the Bedfield 'Crown'. A car pulled up outside, somebody said it was the police and, before I realised what was happening, everybody's glass had been drained and thrown over the bar-counter.

When the young policeman entered, all the tables were empty and there wasn't a glass to be seen, even though the pub's landlord was standing behind the bar ankle-deep in broken glass. There was little the officer-of-the-law could say, apart from, 'Isn't it 'bout time you lot all went home?'

He left, new glasses were refilled and we went on drinking.

David Steele then told me about earlier police visits to the Bedfield 'Crown'.

Must 'ave been a new one. Ain't normal for only one of 'em to come 'ere. Bet some old copper sent him here who knows he'd 'ave troubles.

They've 'ad 'em before. Last time were a few years back. It was just after the old pond and been filled in out front and covered with gravel to make a car-park.

Well, we wus all drinkin' in here on Sat'day night when this car come and this old boy looks through the curtains and says, 'It's the police.' Everybody gets rid of their glasses and waits 'cause the two of them sat out there in their car for a while. Then they comes in and we wus a-sitting there as good as gold.

Well, one old chap who lived at Monk Soham wus a bit bothered 'cause he had no tax on his car. So when they comes in, he goed out through the back way.

These two policemen wus a-lookin' round at us just sittin' there, when this engine starts up. There's a scream of tyres, all this shingle come smashin' ag'in' the windows and then there wus this gre't crash.

Well, we all goes to the windows or the door, just in time to see this old chap drivin' off like a mad man down the road. Then we see he'd smashed straight into the front o' the police car. Well these two policemen rushes out to their car and tries to start it up but the darned thing won't go 'cause the old chap 'ad knocked the fan right into the radiator.

They comes back into the pub and demands to know who'd just driven off but all of us said we didn't know 'cause he didn't come from roundabout 'ere. Well then they 'ad to ring up and wait for another police car to come and fetch 'em.

All that week, they was a-callin' on people what had been in the pub, askin' them questions and that. But they never did find out who'd wrecked their car.

Well, the next Sat'day, just after midnight, a police car comes to the pub ag'in. There was lots and lots of cars in the car-park and this time the police just sit there waitin'. Well, it gets to one o'clock and nothin' is 'appening. Then it gets to two o'clock and they're still sittin' there and nobody's come out of the pub.

Well, at three o'clock in't mornin', the landlord comes out and says, 'Can I help you lads?'

'They says, 'We're waiting for that lot to come out your pub.'

'Well, you've got some bit of a wait,' he says. 'They've all gone to Yarmouth for the day on the coach and left their cars here till they gets back.'

They says, 'So why you've left the pub lights on?'

'Well,' the landlord says, 'I heard a car pull up and I thought it could 'ave been one of them there car thieves. But I reckon it must have been you!'

They policemen didn't believe him and they walks into the pub but it was empty jus like he'd said. So they just had to get back in their car and drive off.

Well, of course, we'd arranged that day-trip special-like, just to make 'em feel a bit silly. We thought that might make 'em come back ag'in the next week, mind. But they didn't.

You see, in the old days, you had a village bobby and he used to come round the back door o' the pub and have a pint hisself. But then they got rid o' him and now you get these smart coppers from Ipswich and that, drivin' around in their fancy cars. They just want to show off a bit. That's all it is.

* * *

Today, of course, there are very few fights in and around village pubs. It has become a socially unacceptable activity that has been crushed by the sometimes excessively heavy hand of the law. There have been many other changes over the years. Most obviously, many pubs have been closed. Debenham, for example, now has two – The Woolpack and The Angel. In the first half of the Twentieth Century, there were another nineteen – The Bucks Head Inn, The Cherry Tree Inn (closed 2008), The Bell, The Dove Inn, The Draper's Arms, The Eight Bell Inn, The Exchequer, The Falcon Inn, The Green Man, The Half Moon, The Joiners Arms, The King's Head Inn, The Queen's Head, The Ram, The Red Lion (closed 1999), The Swan, The Ten Bells, Waterloo House and The White Horse.

The quantity of drink consumed in the surviving public houses has also declined. So too has the amount of time spent in them. Greater prosperity and availability of cars, the smaller size of families and the rightfully increased expectancy of the wives of the surviving farm workers mean that married couples now choose from a much wider variety of entertainment, including, of course, watching television in homes that are far more comfortable and spacious than their parents occupied. The village pub is no longer the place to which a working man goes night after night, leaving his wife at home to look after the children and no household chores now made unnecessary by washing-machines, dish-washers, food mixers and ready-prepared meals.

Most of the village pubs that have survived have become pleasant restaurants catering for visitors from nearby towns clutching a Good Food Guide and for the affluent new village residents who have bought and renovated old country houses and cottages.

Large-scale rural poverty, thankfully, is no more. The old men who sang songs and step-danced in pubs are all dead – and so are their sons. Fortunately, some enthusiastic enthusiasts did record many of the old singers, including Alf Peachey. There are still a few Suffolk pubs that have folk evenings that unfortunately sometimes consist of somewhat pretentious young men and women singing 'traditional' songs.

Sadly, I was not sensible or farsighted enough to record many of the old men I heard singing in Suffolk in the 1970s. I did, however, transcribe with their help some of their songs. A few are in earlier chapters in this book. Here are a few more. I include them not only because they remain my favourites but also because of the differences in these lyrics to other published versions.

* * *

THE BLACK VELVET BAND

Although this song, like many others sung in Suffolk pubs, is a warning to men about the dangers of city life and associating with 'loose women', it is also about a young man being transported to Van Diemen's Land (now Tasmania) for committing a trivial crime, such as 'receiving a stolen chicken'. It was a common, life-changing experience endured by many. Between 1800 and 1853, 1,969 people from Suffolk were transported to Van Diemen's Land for periods ranging from 3 years to life. Some did not survive the four-month voyage.

During the same period, many Suffolk parishes, under the New Poor law, funded a scheme for the emigration to Australia of unemployed farm-labourers and their families. In the twelve months from June 1835, 787 Suffolk emigrants were sent from 32 parishes.

'Twas in the city of London
in 'prenticeship I was bound
and many's the gay old hour

I've spent in that dear old town.
One day as I was a-walking
along my usual beat,
I spied a pretty young maiden
come tripping along the street.
  Chorus
    Her eyes they shone like diamonds.
    I thought her the queen of the land.
    And her hair it hung over her shoulders,
    tied up with a black velvet band.

One day as we were a-walking,
a gentleman passed us by.
I could tell she was up to some mischief
by the look in her dark blue eyes.
Gold watch she took from his pocket
and slyly placed in my hand.
I was taken in charge by a copper.
Bad luck to the black velvet band.
  Chorus

Before the Lord Mayor I was taken:
'Your case, sir, I plainly can see,
and, if I'm not too much mistaken,
you're bound far off over sea,
far over the dark and blue ocean,
far away to the Van Dieman's Land,
far away from your friends and relations
and the girl with the black velvet band.'
  Chorus
    Her eyes they shone like diamonds.
    I thought her the queen of the land.
    And her hair it hung over her shoulders,
    tied up with a black velvet band.

* * *

THE YELLOW HANDKERCHIEF

This is an old song, probably dating from the 1850s and possibly originating in Ireland. Suffolk versions of the song are very different from most others that tell of a young woman's loves and has the alternative title of 'First I loved William and then I loved John'. The Suffolk song deals with a young man losing his love by associating with 'flash company'.

My friend, John Ridgard, suggested to me that the reason for the long-term popularity of the Suffolk version is that it provides a heavily disguised comment on the long-remembered, disastrous effects suffered by farm labourers in 1874. Joseph Arch, who had founded the National Agricultural Workers' Union two years earlier, organised a strike in Suffolk and North Essex seeking higher wages for labourers. By the beginning of April, over 6,000 men were on strike.

It was broken by a lockout of union members by farmers who formed the Essex and Suffolk Farmers' Defence Association, who declared that they would not pay more than 2s for a twelve-hour day and would sack workers who would not agree to leave the union. In May, the 'Ipswich Journal' reported that 1,250 men were being paid strike pay by the union: 341 in Saxmundham, 576 in Woodbridge, 117 in Botesdale, 150 in Stowmarket, 44 in Westhorpe and 22 in Elmswell.

As harvest time approached, some workers were allowed to go back to work but Arch reported that 4,000 men had permanently lost their jobs, leading to considerable poverty, migration to the towns or emigration to Australia or Canada. It also led to considerable and a long continuing distrust between workers and farm-owners.

'The Yellow Handkerchief' was, John Ridgard believed, a coded account of the events that could safely be sung in public. 'Yellow' was the political colour of the Liberal Party that, in rural Suffolk as elsewhere in England, was the established opposition to the Conservative Party which was supported by most Suffolk landowners and represented the rural areas of the county throughout the Nineteenth Century. Yellow was, therefore, an acceptable colour of opposition, however much it might have irritated the local landowners.

'Flash Company' consisted of the members of the union during the strike that 'ruined my life'.

The concluding verse starts:
'Once I had a colour as red as a rose.
Now I'm as pale as the lily that grows.'
'Red' was the revolutionary colour worn by the strikers. For the singer, it was a colour he could wear no more.

With the collapse of the strike and the disastrous effects of the lockout, the singer no longer has a political colour or a future and so he advises his girlfriend and everybody else to wear the acceptable protest colour of 'yellow' in order to remember him and be aware of his misfortunes. By belonging to the Agricultural Workers' Union, he had lost his job and, therefore, his girl.

> Once I loved a young girl as I love my life.
> Keeping her in flash company has ruined my life.
> It's ruined my life like a great many more.
> Hadn't been for flash company, I'd never been poor.

Chorus
Take the yellow handkerchief in remembrance of me.
Wear it round your neck, love, in flash company -
flash company, my boys, like a great many more.
Hadn't have been for flash company,
  I'd never been so poor.

Fiddlin' and a-dancin' was all my delight.
Keeping her in flash company had ruined my life.
It's ruined my life like a great many more.
Hadn't been for flash company, I'd never been poor.
  Chorus

Once I had a colour, as red as a rose.
Now I'm as pale as the lily that grows.
Like a flower in the garden my colour has gone.
You can see what I'm comin' to for love of that one.
  Chorus
  Take the yellow handkerchief in remembrance of me.
  Wear it round your neck, love, in flash company -
  flash company, my boys, like a great many more.
  Hadn't have been for flash company,
    I'd never been so poor.

The Thatcher

Russell Podd – born 1925

In the early part of the Twentieth Century, in every Suffolk village there were several craftsmen, including the saddler, basket maker, blacksmith, thatcher, carpenter, baker, butcher, cheese-maker, dressmaker, shoe-repairer, locksmith, pharmacist and chimney-sweep. As the demand for the services rapidly declined, almost all of them have disappeared from the countryside. An exception is the thatcher whose specialist skills are still much in demand. The origins of the craft date back over 4,500 years to the Bronze Age.

In 1980, I spoke to the highly praised thatcher, Russell Podd. He left school in 1939, at the age of fourteen, and went straight into the family thatching business that had been founded by his great-grandfather.

Apart from a few years spent in the Army, he was always a

thatcher and, as many beautifully thatched houses in Suffolk bear witness, he had an immense love and knowledge of his craft.

Russell Podd

To find the right straw for thatching, you first have to find a farmer in the mind to help you. Most wheat grown now is short-strawed but there are about six or seven varieties still grown that are suitable. I prefer to work with Maris Widgeon or Maris Guntsman which is a new one that's a bit on the fine side. You see, for thatching, you mustn't have pithy straw. It must be a long straw that's hollow.

The next thing is to persuade the farmer not to use too much nitrogen on the wheat, 'cause nitrogen makes it rot up that much quicker. And it's no good putting growth regulator on it, 'cause you must let it grow full size.

For cutting, you have to use a self-binder. They're pretty rare now and so I've got one of my own. The wheat's cut when the straw is a bit on the green side. Then it's stood up into stooks in the field for a week to ten days, so the grain can harden and ripen.

The wheat's then taken to an old-fashioned threshing-machine that takes off all the grain and the chaff. You're left with the loose straw which you put into a big stack on the farmer's land. The farmer's happy enough with the arrangement, 'cause the young people don't know how to use the machinery and they just won't be told. So that causes a problem. Still we help the farmer a lot. We do all the cutting and binding, load up the trailers and help with the threshing.

Mind, the straw still costs five times more than the straw from the combine – and the farmer keeps all the grain. Course, if the farmer doesn't have his own threshing-machine, you can't do anything. So I'm just going to have to buy my own.

But, as a thatcher, I'm used to that. When I have a trainee, the first thing he's got to do is buy or make his own tools. We never use each other's. So that makes thatchers very protective of their equipment. You've got to have the tools because otherwise you can't work.

It's no good coming on Monday morning and saying, 'I've lost me thatching needles. Can I borrow yours?'

The answer will be a straight, 'No!' You either find your own or you go without.

When you come to thatch, everything is done on the site. With straw, there's a lot of work involved, even though you just re-case the thatch – apart from the ridge on top which is new every time. You only rake off any of the old thatch that's rotten. You don't strip the rest off.

So some of the straw thatch on a house had been there for two or three hundred years - perhaps even longer than that. Each time it's thatched, it just has another layer put on top.

After the new straw's been brought to the site, it's laid out and soaked with water. Then it's shaken up into a bed. From the bottom of the bed, you pull out a 'yealm' – a bundle of straw. The yealms are then put onto a 'yoke', which is a carrying device that takes nine or ten yealms. The yoke is then carried up to the roof.

You can start in either direction but I always prefer to work from right to left. You start at the bottom of the eves and you lay a yealm vertically on top of the old, cleaned thatch.

Each yealm is held by 'broaches'. Now these are made from hazel. You buy in the wood and cut it down into two-foot lengths which are riven up into as many broaches as it comes.

You can get two, four, six, eight or even twelve broaches out of a length of hazel. Each one is then pointed at both ends with a special 'billhook' and then it's twisted in the middle so it makes a kind of staple. You drive that with a mallet through the new straw into the old thatch underneath.

You work in courses, starting from the bottom and then up to the top. Each yealm is overlapped about half way and then it's broached. You put four broaches into each yealm. You lift up each yealm in the course below with thatching needles so you can catch on to each section as you go up. That's the art of thatching – joining up so that none of the joints or courses show.

When all the roof is covered, you do the ridge, which is the ornamental part. You put the ridge on by laying straw on top of the straw you've already laid so that it's raised up.

SWEET SORREL

Some goes right over the top and over the other side, being held on with hazel-rods which go long-ways parallel to the ridge.

Then you make whatever ornamental pattern you want with rods, all carefully measured out. Just below the rods, you cut the straw with special sheers so that the ridge stands out. That adds the unique look to thatch. Almost every thatcher has his own ridge design. Also, in Suffolk, it's traditional to have peaked ends – that is the ridge runs straight to the ends and then it's pealed out instead of being rounded off.

When that's finished, you soak the whole roof with water. You either carry it up in pails or use a hosepipe, which we always do if we can. Then we have a special comb or rake with willow teeth with which we comb the whole thing down while it's wet. That makes the straw lay perfectly flat.

Next, you have the eaves to contend with. You have an eaves knife, which is a long blade, and you put a board on the eave under your ladder and you cut the straw over the eaves at a slight angle. Then we run a rod along the bottom of that, held by broaches, just to stop the wind getting under it.

The last job is to put the wire-netting on. We used to put it right over the top but now we start at the top and drop it down one side at a time. It used to be attached with what we called 'lacing-wire' but we use a different method now that really the fire-brigade thought up.

The edges of the wire, where they overlap, are twisted together with a special tool which sort of brings one over the top of the other. The idea is that, in case of fire, they can get to the seat of it quickly because, if you get hold at the bottom and give it a sharp tug, it'll come undone.

We take the wire right underneath the eave and nail it at the back. The nails are always bent back to make it easier to get the netting off.

There's now a nylon net that I think is probably going to take over from the galvanised wire-netting. You can't break it and it's much lighter. But, at the moment, we still use the old wire-netting.

That's basically the straw thatching. It takes about a month to cover the roof and then another couple of weeks to do the ridge and comb out. Course, a layman doing the ridge would take a lot longer but, when you get used to it, you can cut them without making a lot of measurements.

There's a tremendous demand now from people wanting thatching. My average estimate now of the waiting time before I can do a job is two and a half years. It's been like that since 1970. Before that, I was going more or less from one job to another. But there's a lot of interest in thatching now. I've had people who've had all the tiles taken off their houses and thatch put on instead. Then they told me that it had cut the heating bills by half – it's such a good insulator. You see a recoated straw rood could be anything from eighteen inches to four feet deep.

But this demand for thatching means there's a lot of cowboys about now which is doing a tremendous amount of harm. They sort of go with a thatcher for about six months and think they know it all. Then they get a job and botch it. And that's not good for other thatchers. I had a case recently where a so-called thatcher charged a customer twice the proper cost. But that's the kind of thing that's happening. I've been called in a dozen times to deal with bad workmanship but there not much one can do. When it's been messed up, you can't put it right. It's just got to be done all over again.

CORN DOLLIES

In Suffolk, as in many other rural areas throughout the world, it was believed that the spirit of the Harvest Goddess lived in the fields and that, as the reapers cut the corn, the spirit was forced to retreat until it was lodged in the last remaining strand of corn. So, in order not to drive away the spirit, the last sheaf was twisted roughly into the shape of a woman and decorated with coloured ribbons. This corn dolly would then be kept in the farmhouse over the winter and then ploughed into the land the following spring.

In time, much smaller hollow shapes, plaited from strands of corn, were made instead and each area acquired its own particular form. In Suffolk, it was a horseshoe, commemorating the importance there had been in the county, before mechanization, of the Suffolk Punch and the horsemen who worked with them.

Today, their original purpose ignored, a variety of intricate corn dollies are used to decorate the farmhouse and the church, both at harvest time and for weddings.

Mrs Peacock of Earl Soham spoke to me about the making of corn dollies.

The best straw to use comes from a very old variety of wheat which is not grown commercially. It's off the Ministry of Agriculture list purely because the yield is so bad but it has a long straw from the ear to the first joint or node. You can't get that nowadays in modern wheat, because they breed them short for the combine harvester.

The old wheat is called Masterpiece and it's sometimes five or six feet high when it's growing and it has red ears. The best white ear is called Elite. These are the two that I use and both are now grown specifically for making corn dollies.

It's cut about three weeks before harvest. That's when the ear is still upright and before it's really ripe. So you get some green down by the first node. It has to be cut with a binder, not a combine, because it mustn't be squashed. So sometimes you just have to cut it by hand, which you do at ground level.

After you bring the straw home, you have to dry it out, which means opening up the bundles of straw and leaving it out on a nice, hot sunny day, then turning it over at mid-day, and then tying it up again in the evening and putting it back in the shed. It takes three or four hours of that to dry it out completely. If you leave it tied up in a bundle, it goes moldy because it's green and it's sappy. Then you get a very black, moldy straw.

When it's dried, it's completely white. You then put it out of the reach of mice, rats and the weather. I've got it up in the summerhouse. Then, when you've got a couple of hours to spare, you get your sheaf of straw and a blanket and you strip it out. This entails cutting the ear off and then cutting again just above the first node. The flag (or leaf) is the stripped off.

So the pieces you use for weaving are from between the ear and the first node. Each one is cut individually. You cannot cut them together because no two are the same length. I use scissors and cut the ear off at an angle because, when you're joining straws, it's easier to insert the narrower end if it's angled than if it's flat. Above the node, it's cut straight. So it's angled at the top and straight at the bottom. If you've got a good ear, you keep it because you need some ears for decoration and so those you leave in the stalk. All the others, you grade into thicknesses – large, medium and small. All that means you've got many hours' work before you start!

When you're ready to make a corn dolly, you first soak the straw you're going to use in cold water for twenty or thirty minutes. This makes it more pliable. I put mine in the sink with a towel on top, because it tends to float up to the surface. Then, while I'm working, the straw is kept wrapped in the damp towel.

Next, you get together the other things you need. You must have sharp scissors and fawn-coloured thread. (I use carpet-linen thread because you have to tie the straw very tightly because it shrinks when it dries.)

Then you must have some coloured ribbon to decorate the finished dolly with a bow. Traditionally, only five colours are used – red for the poppy, blue for the cornflower, green for the rebirth of the seed, white for purity and gold for the goddess and the colour of the grain.

Postscript

There are three aspects of village life that, although they often dominate accounts of rural English counties, are rarely mentioned in this book. They are the church, the school and the landowners.

Until the Second World War, there were still some Suffolk villages that were fiefdoms of rich and powerful squires who were the major local employer and owner of most of the village housing. Rich and often ruthless, they wielded their considerable power not only locally but also much further afield. Throughout the nineteenth century, when most of the population did not have the vote, Suffolk elected as MPs a series of Tory, aristocratic landowners, including the Lord Henniker (an Irish peer), Sir Edward Gooche, The Lord Rendleham (another Irish peer), and Viscount Mahon.

Local landowners also exercised what at times was total control over the local church, school and political life.

As their families had done for generations, many Suffolk

gentry owned an 'advowson' that gave them the right to nominate the vicar for the local church - subject to the approval of the local Bishop. The local church might well have been constructed and for centuries maintained by the family. Some of them were celebrated inside with elaborate tombs and memorials. At the front of the church, there were often elaborately carved pews that were reserved for the exclusive use of the squire and his family. (There were also some churches that had a gallery at the west end reserved for 'the servants and underprivileged'!)

In the closed, feudal villages, church attendance of tenants and workers was obligatory. One of the biggest Suffolk landowners had a rule, even in the early 1930s, that 'all tenants, their wife and children must attend church each Sunday wearing clothes appropriate to their station and not above it'!

Not surprisingly, the farm labourers who did not work for the village squire and the local tradesmen and shop workers were rarely established church attenders. Hector More related a conversation that Frank Ablett, then the publican in Brandeston, had with the local vicar:

Poor old Frank Ablett used to go to church once a year for Harvest Thanksgiving. And he always used to put a pound on the plate and when he put it in he'd say in a loud voice, 'There! That's me and the Lord square for the year!'

Well, we had a new parson and he came just before Harvest Thanksgiving and seeing the publican in church that pleased him. But, of course, for several weeks he didn't see him no more and he met Frank in the village one day.

'Haven't seen you at church, Mr Ablett,' he says.

'No, sir! No, sir!' he says. 'But you haven't lost me custom. I en't been anywhere else!'

* * *

The village public house was, even in closed villages, one of the rare places that were totally independent of the squire. Hence, their popularity with working men!

Most village institutions, including the local school, did not enjoy such independence.

Until 1870, all schools in England were charitable or private institutions. In rural areas, there was little educational provision for village children. Some schools had been built either by the Church of England or by large landowners on their land. For example, Helmingham School was built on the Tollemache estate and opened in 1853. At first, it had two parts. The Upper School was for the sons or farmers and professional men. The Lower School was for the boys and girls of farm workers.

The Elementary Education Act of 1870 created the idea of compulsory education for children aged 5 to 10. The schools in rural areas were to be run by an elected School Board. The new law had little effect on many rural areas in Suffolk where there were no schools for the children to attend. Even where schools did exist, exemptions were granted for illness and living more than a mile from a school.

Because of the mass abandonment of villages that followed the 1874/5 lockouts, there was a heavy demand for cheap child labour that impoverished parents could not resist. So young boys continued, as they had always done, to work in the fields and girls became servants or shop assistants.

Partially in an attempt to prevent landowners and others employing children who should have been at school, the Elementary Education Act of 1880 insisted on compulsory education from 5-10 years. However, it also introduced a Labour Certificate that permitted pupils to leave school earlier if they had reached a satisfactory standard. In 1893, the school leaving age was raised to 11 and later 13.

Enforcing attendance proved very difficult and, of course, impossible in areas where there was no school. In rural areas, the problem was not resolved until the passing of Balfour's Education Act in 1902 that established in England and Wales a single system that united all local schools funded by ratepayers and run by elected school boards with the 14,000 voluntary schools, funded nationally and operated by the Church of England and the Catholic Church. School boards were abolished and all elementary schools came under the control of the newly established Local Education Authorities.

It mattered not whether the village school was run by a school board, the Church or the LEAs, the large landowners, either personally or through their nominees, often exerted considerable control over local schools, staff appointments and what was taught.

Compulsory schooling created many difficulties in rural areas because the nearest school could be several miles away. David Peachey lived in Framsden and attended Helmingham School, nearly three miles away.

I started there when I was five and it seemed a terrible long way to walk. There was no mistake about that. I never thought I was goin' to reach the school. I used very often to fall asleep in school.

Every day I had to walk but, as we came from a poor family, clothes were very limited. The first few years, I used to wear my two elder sisters' shoes what they had grown out of. I did that practically all the time. They were button shoes and one day when I got to school these boys cut the buttons off and, as they were bigger then me, I couldn't say nothin' about it.

I used to sit at home in the evenin' and pray for rain so that I shouldn't have to go to school the next day.

(In the 1970s, two of my sons went to Helmingham Primary School - the same school David Peachy had attended. It was still in the same building – and a very good school it was!)

In 1918, the school leaving age was raised to 14. Up to then, it was still possible for boys and girls to obtain a Labour Certificate that permitted them to leave school earlier. (In 1918, my mother was given one of them and started work in a Lancashire cotton mill at the age of 12.) In rural Suffolk, certificates seem to have been instantly given if requested or when the teacher wanted to get rid of a troublesome student.

This is Cooker Carver's account of how he left Earl Soham School.

Mr Rice was our schoolmaster and there were a lot of us boys worked up at the allotment. Rice was in the potting-shed and one of these old boys says to me, 'Cooker, you dussn't lock old Rice in the hut!'

So I said, 'I bloody-well duss!'

So I went and shut the door, gave the key a turn and left Rice in there. Course, he thought the door had a-blown to.

Well we went all home and he was there till five o'clock till some 'un heard him holler.

But the buggers split on me. Next mornin' when I went to school, old Rice said, 'Come on, Carver. I want some drill from you.'

I said, 'Oh! What 'ave I done now?'

He said, 'You know what you done. Locked me in that shed!'

I said, 'I didn't!'

'You did,' he said. 'Now you can do some drillin' in front of the school.'

So out I went and he told me to put me arms up and sideways stretch and all that. Then he said, 'Touch yer toes.' Well I never gave it a thought but he'd got a cane in his hand. I stretched and touched me toes and he cut me in the arse with his cane.

Well I runned home out the school and he shouted after me, 'You can stop at home too. We don't want you here no more. You're a bloody nuisance!'

That's how I come to leave school. They sent the papers through and that was that. And a bloody good job too!

* * *

Today, many of the old village schools have closed and the buildings have been converted into expensive houses. Village churches remain but many are only historic monuments because there is no local vicar or regular services. The landed gentry have long lost the powers that once they regarded as their right. Some of the large landholdings have been broken up and sold to independent farmers.

Times they are a-changing – but so they have always been. There never was a golden age of country life when everything was perfect – nor will there ever be. The farmer and the labourers know that a week's rain at the right time can produce a bumper harvest, just as an unwanted drought can bring disaster. So the uncontrollable elements, rather than the apparently uncontrollable state of the national economy, are still the major concern of those that farm. It is perhaps this, more than anything else, which separates the rural from the urban people.

What contentment the declining number of agricultural workers have in their working lives comes not from a ruthless acquisition of wealth but from the experience of successfully pitting themselves daily against the elements and reaping the good harvest as well as the bad.

ABOUT THE AUTHOR

Sydney Higgins has been a successful writer for many years. When Cassell published his first book, the managing director insisted that his name should be changed to 'D.S. Higgins' because, he said, 'Sydney Higgins sounds common'! He went on to write over 40 educational books for the publisher before writing his first biography. Later books, published by other companies, appeared under the names 'Sydney Higgins' and 'Syd Higgins'.

Then, after being appointed to be a Senior Inspector of English and Drama in Suffolk (UK), the name he used for writing became unimportant because, as he was not permitted to publish anything under his own name - whether it was 'D.S.', 'Sydney' or 'Syd' - he became a ghost writer and was the author of several books including *Stroll On* for Tony Booth, *Piper Alpha - A Survivor's Story* for Ed Punchard, *The Pirelli Book of Motor Racing Heroes* for John Surtees and *Nicola: A Second Chance to Live* for Nicola Owen.

In the early 1990s, he and his wife, who is also a writer, moved to Italy. There he became a Professor of English, spending much time studying medieval drama and writing sure-fire slow-sellers on subjects such as *The Staging of Cornish Medieval Drama*. He also founded and still directs his own theatrical company that specialises in musicals, including several for which he has written the book and the lyrics. He and his wife love travelling and together have written a two-part guidebook, *Staying in the Châteaux Hotels of France.*

In 2000, he was made the 'Citizen of the Year' in the Italian town where he lives and works.

Printed in Great Britain
by Amazon.co.uk, Ltd.,
Marston Gate.